JULIAN APPLEBY

LOLO CASTAGNOLA

JESUS 'PELON' ELOY
ESCAPITE

MILO FERNANDEZ-ARAUJO

MIGUEL NOVILLO ASTRADA

WILLIAM LUCAS

SANTIAGO TORREGUITAR

GUILLERMO 'MEMO' GRACIDA

ANDREA VIANINI

TOM MORLEY

CARLOS GRACIDA

ALFIO MARCHINI

NICHOLAS DE LISLE

PASCUAL SAINZ DE VICUÑA

SANTIAGO ARAYA

SEBASTIAN DAWNAY

JOHN PAUL CLARKIN

ALEJANDRO 'NEGRO'
NOVILLO ASTRADA

FRED MANNIX

GEORGE MILFORD HAVEN

DIEGO ARAYA

STEVE CROWDER

EDUARDO 'RUSO' HEGUY

ROBERT BALLARD

CLAIRE TOMLINSON

VIERI ANTINORI

MAREK A. DOCHNAL

HOWARD JOHN HIPWOOD

IGNACIO 'NACHO' DOMECQ

JAMES BEIM

MICHAEL GREGORY TODD

RYAN CONROY

VISIONS

— OF —

POLO

VISIONS
— OF —
POLO

ELIZABETH
FURTH

KENILWORTH PRESS

British Library Cataloguing-in-Publication Data.
A catalogue record for this book is available from the
British Library.

ISBN 1-872119-92-1

Published by Kenilworth Press Ltd, Addington,
Buckingham, Bucks, MK18 2JR

Designed by design principals, Warminster, England.
Colour separation by Tien Wah Press. Singapore
Printed by Tien Wah Press, Singapore.

**Previous page: USA player at speed during the F.I.P. World
Championships, Chantilly, September 2004.**

CONTENTS

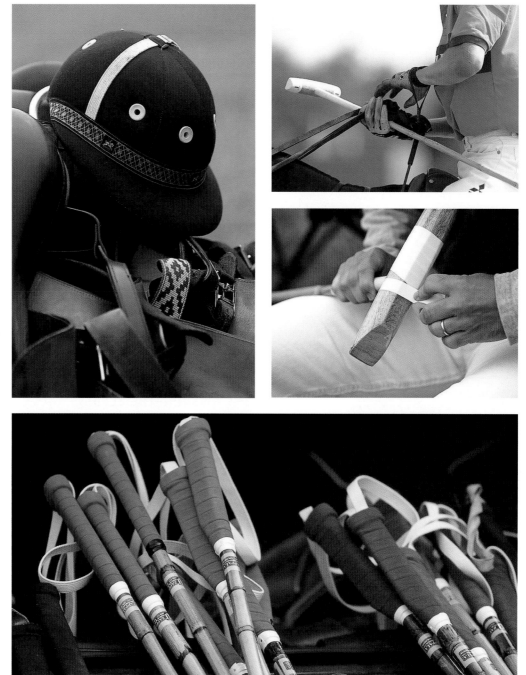

(Right) Guards 2003.

(Far right, top) Luke Tomlinson,
Beaufort Polo Club 2003.

(Far right, bottom) J. Hernan
Rivas, Ellerston 2004.

(Right) Cirencester 2003.

ACKNOWLEDGEMENTS

Firstly I would like to thank Urs Schwarzenbach, patron of Black Bears and his wife Francesca; without their help and backing this book would not have happened. Travelling all around the world and collecting the material for *Visions of Polo* was only possible because of their generous support. My thanks also go to Jane Paterson, secretary of Black Bears. Not only did Jane organize all my trips around the world so efficiently, but she has also always been a friendly and supportive voice on the other end of the telephone. A big thank you goes to Black Bears' manager Doug McGregor for supporting the concept of *Visions of Polo* and for initially presenting the idea to Urs.

Thank you to the friendly and efficient team at Sky Photographic, in particular Debbie Wells and Sylvia Kentish, for their encouragement.

I am very grateful to Safdar Zaman, team leader at Canon UK for doing his best to keep my cameras ticking over, and to Alejandra Falkinhoff, director of Argentine Trading and the brain behind the ONA products, for her kind help.

My thanks also go to the designer Graham Webb for being open to learning about the subtleties of polo, and to my editor Jane Lake for her excellence.

I owe gratitude to Daisaku Ikeda and the Nichiren Buddhism I practise for showing me that the biggest victory is over oneself.

Last and by no means least a big thank you goes to all the polo players who kindly allowed me into their world; it is they and their polo ponies who inspired me to produce this book.

Dedication

For my family and all the people who are in my heart;
their love, humour and support means the world to me!

HRH Prince Charles
receiving his prize from
Her Majesty the Queen,
after the Gulf Co-operation
Council Day (GCC) at
Guards Polo Club, 2003.

(Right) HRH Prince Charles
during an exhibition match
at Guards Polo Club, 2003.

CLARENCE HOUSE

I am delighted to write a foreword for Elizabeth Furth's book which so graphically describes the true essence of Polo.

I think the photographs not only depict the unrivalled skill, drama, teamwork and huge fun which is unique to Polo, but they also turn images into an art form. Moreover, Elizabeth's interviewing ability clearly encourages an openness in both professional players and patrons that allow the reader to be part of their intimate world.

Having been lucky enough to play Polo for over 40 years, I am sure Visions of Polo will provide a frequent reminder to us of why we are so passionate about the game and I do congratulate the author on producing such a fine work of art.

PREFACE

Since my books *Visions of Show Jumping*, *Visions of Eventing* and *Visions of Dressage* have been published, I have had a strong desire to produce a similar book on polo in order to try to capture the essence of this wonderfully exciting sport photographically. The images in *Visions of Polo* are complemented by interviews with numerous polo players and other people connected with polo, and I have aspired to offer the reader a true representation of the polo world.

During the one and a half years it has taken me to put this book together, I discovered that people whose lives revolve around hitting a ball while travelling at considerable speed on board a horse transcend all social barriers.

Highly successful businessmen, who are the patrons of most teams, polo professionals and grooms, all pull together to make polo possible. They gather together socially, having a good time and sharing polo anecdotes until the cows come home!

I wished to dedicate a chapter to the ins and outs of running a successful polo organization, and had the good fortune and pleasure to meet two highly successful patrons: Hubert Perrodo, patron of Labegorce, and Ali Albwardi, patron of Dubai. Both men are very different in many ways and yet their passion for horses and the taxing game of polo brings them together in more than one way.

Selecting just one candidate from many, many talented players, to describe what makes someone dedicate their life to polo and become a top player, was no easy choice. But, talking to ten-goal player, Argentine Adolfo Cambiaso, has taught me that talent, determination, passion, humbleness, team spirit and a touch of genius is what it takes to be at the top of this sport.

Strong family bonds are very apparent in polo and, wishing to pursue this topic, I have devoted a chapter to siblings. Meeting English brothers Luke and Mark Tomlinson and the five brothers of the Argentine Novillo-Astrada clan, emphasized the fact that having players who share genes on the same team seems to be a vital ingredient for success.

By meeting and talking to all these highly gifted polo players, I have not only acquired a deeper understanding of what drives their passion, but it has also thrown light on the complexity of the sport.

Taking the photographs for *Visions of Polo* has been a huge challenge but I brought a love for detail, action and horses to the project, and I did know what I wanted to capture. Punchy photos full of drama, expression and harmony between horse and rider is what I mostly set out to achieve, but truly succeeding in capturing all of this can prove to be very difficult! With polo, more than with any of the other equestrian disciplines I have photographed, success lies mainly in being at the right place at the right time. But, with the polo field being three times as big as a football field plus the added restriction to access – owing to a certain element of danger from flying balls and horses moving at speed – securing good photos was not as straightforward as one might think!

Knowing the game to the extent I do helped somewhat in choosing good positions from which I wanted to shoot the photographs, but the six-million-dollar question remained: where would the action and the play really be once the matches were in full swing? Would it be behind the goalmouth or more or less in the middle of the field? The answer is yes on both accounts but knowing *when* was still an unknown factor, particularly as teams change ends after each scored goal. So, with a bit of bad luck, all the action could easily be happening at the 'wrong' end of the field all match long. And if fortune was on my side, I could be blessed with great action all match long. One thing I learned pretty fast was that as soon as you change ends because you think that the action is always happening at the other end, the action will also have switched, which effectively means that you will be in the same predicament as before! Praying is one way to attract good action to your spot; being patient is the other.

The idea of thinking 'the longer the lens the better the chances of catching the action' does not necessarily apply either. High-goal polo moves at such an incredible pace that, one second my frame could be filled with action, and the next the image would either have moved out of my reach or be filling my frame too much! The perfect shot happening just in front of you with the right light, crisp framing and exciting action, all in the viewfinder, ready to be snapped, is a rare occurrence; and so when it all falls into place, photographing polo is both very exciting and most rewarding!

Travelling around the world following high-goal polo was a lot of fun too. I consider myself very lucky to have had the opportunity to visit exquisite places such as Garangula and Ellerston in Australia. Flying to Buenos Aires for the Argentine Open meant that I was able to witness polo at its best, and being there for three weeks also meant that I was able to visit the street in Buenos Aires where my grandmother, who I sadly never met, had lived and died.

Photographing high-goal polo on the frozen lake of St. Moritz, Switzerland, will remain an unforgettable experience, and being in

Javier Novillo-Astrada on the attack during the subsidiary semi-final of the 2004 Sotogrande Gold Cup.

Florida for the US Open allowed me to photograph polo players who don't necessarily make it to England.

In England I concentrated on the Queen's Cup, the Warwickshire Cup, the Gold Cup and the European Championships. In France I covered the Deauville Gold Cup and the F.I.P. World Championships, which took place in Chantilly, and in Spain I went to Sotogrande for their Gold Cup.

It has been my ambition to create a book about polo for polo enthusiasts from around the world to enjoy, but I hope it will also open a window on the sport for newcomers.

Juan José 'JJ' Diaz Alberdi has been a professional umpire for more than ten years.

'It all started in Argentina when one day I was asked to help out.' JJ is the older brother of Alejandro 'Piki' Diaz Alberdi and is now the manager of Marek Dochnal's newly founded Larchmont polo team. JJ has been involved in polo all his life. He is still a five-goal player and enjoys playing low- and medium-goal polo.

UMPIRING AND THE 'THIRD MAN'

All those who have watched a polo match are, no doubt, attracted by the immense speed involved in the game. Two four-player teams charge fast and furiously up and down a field three times the size of a football pitch, trying to score goals at either end of that field.

Regulating the event are two mounted umpires who are not only trying to keep up with the action (often on slower horses than the players) but, more to the point, are also there to ensure that the game is played fairly and runs smoothly. They can be easily recognized by their attire, usually a black and white polo shirt and a helmet of matching colours. They are also equipped with a pick-up stick to pick up loose polo balls, a leather ball bag attached to the saddle in front of the pommel – containing spare polo balls – and a whistle.

Should the two riding umpires not agree on any matter, they will seek the opinion of a third umpire referred to as the 'third man'. He usually sits up in the stands alongside the polo field, as high up as possible in order to get an excellent overall view of the game in progress.

Nowadays, matches played during the English high-goal season, as well as other important tournaments around the world, are arbitrated by a team of professional umpires. In England it is a team

of ten employed by the Hurlingham Polo Association (H.P.A.). You will, however, still find tournaments where umpiring duties are given to players entered in those very tournaments but, out of all the events I have covered for *Visions of Polo*, I recall only three: the Deauville Gold Cup tournament and the two Australian tournaments in Ellerston and Garangula. At these tournaments, organizers draw the umpires from the pool of players in order to get every player to umpire at least once during the tournament.

When speaking to players who have been assigned the duties of umpiring, I found the overriding feeling to be that they don't really enjoy it but only do it because it is

Queen's Cup 2003.

part of the regulations of a particular tournament's organizing committee. Their reservations are understandable, particularly as more often than not players would have to umpire a match between teams they themselves will have to play throughout the tournament. And, in the heat of the moment, an agitated player might accuse the umpire of not being impartial enough. Pepe Araya, for example, is a player

Umpire Andrew Seavill just
about to throw the ball back
into play.

who says that he doesn't enjoy it at all. He recalls his duties in Deauville as being 'Quite difficult, especially because I had to umpire matches my friends were playing in: people I play with or against all the time. I really prefer playing.'

Chilean Gabriel Donoso, still an active high-goal player, gets asked to umpire quite a lot. He has in the past even been asked to do so during the Argentine Open. More recently Gabriel was asked to umpire the 2003 Coronation Cup on Cartier Day. He does not take the job lightly. He finds it to be quite a big responsibility and points out that his main aim is 'to do a good job for both teams and not to upset any players'. Adding to that Gabriel thinks that professional umpires are doing a good job especially as they don't get involved in arguments with players.

For polo players who no longer take part in high-goal tournaments, umpiring can be quite rewarding. It allows them to keep their eye in, to feel the excitement of a competition, to still be part of the polo scene and to enjoy the way of life they so love. English professional umpire Paul Withers, a very accomplished polo player for many years while playing for Lord Cowdray, sees umpiring as a way of staying involved in the sport he adores.

Howard Hipwood, one of England's best polo players and a nine-goaler in his day says, half smiling, that he is 'working on enjoying being a professional umpire!' One thing he is quite clear about, however, is that he is totally unbiased. This makes him very well respected and liked amongst players. 'I read the play as I see it and the players know that.'

New Zealander Tim Keyte, father of Simon Keyte, has for seven years been part of the team of ten professional umpires the H.P.A. employs. He too finds the job very challenging as well as a lot of fun.

Umpire Paul Withers having a quiet moment before umpire duties.

Paul, winner of numerous cups including the Gold Cup in 1969, gave up playing polo in 1995 and has made the transition to professional umpire since then. 'I was going to be a professional cricketer but as soon as I started hitting a polo ball that was the end of cricket!'

And, in his charming kiwi accent he told me, 'I'd say I get the best seat in the house to watch a high-goal match from.' And, on a more serious note, Tim explained that the semi-finals of any high-goal tournament are the most difficult matches to umpire. 'You have to be twice as sharp as everything counts for both teams.'

Although Howard Hipwood never really stopped playing polo, followers of high-goal polo will see him umpiring a lot during the English summer months.

Howard has won four Queen's Cup titles. He has also been in numerous Gold Cup finals and has won the trophy once.

'Polo has almost been like a mother to me. It has looked after me all my life and has never let me down. As for umpiring, I am working on enjoying it! One thing is for sure, I am totally unbiased which is why people like me. I read the game as I see it and players know that.'

The Australian high-goal player Glen Gilmore is fanatical about the game and the rules of polo. At present he has taken on the task of rewriting the Australian rule book. Glen finds getting involved in the rules exhilarating because he wants to try to guide the game more towards opening up. In his eyes, 'This would make the game both faster and more thrilling for players and spectators.'

To throw more light on the ins and outs of the game of polo and the accompanying criteria, I spoke to Chief Umpire Robert Graham. He is in charge of the group of ten professional umpires working in England during the polo season.

Robert Graham

Should you ever be looking for Robert Graham in the course of a polo match during the English high-goal season, your best bet is to make your way to the stands where he will be acting as the third man, the arbiter between the two umpires out on the polo field. However, Robert's official title and main job for the Hurlingham Polo Association (H.P.A.) is 'Chief Umpire' a position he claims he was only given because: 'I can't be employed anywhere else really!' It is clear though that the job makes great demands on Robert and is very time consuming as he has to be present at all major matches where professional umpires are at work. Robert took over as Chief Umpire in 2004 when his predecessor Douglas Newgent stepped down because 'Douglas wanted more time to do other things.' The job does not come with an officially established timescale.

Robert Graham, Chief Umpire of the Hurlingham Polo Association (H.P.A.) on duty during a league match played at Black Bears' polo grounds in Shiplake. On this occasion Robert was also acting as third man. Radio in hand, Robert can immediately be in direct communication with the two umpires on the field should they need his advice.

'The purpose of the radio is to keep things moving. They are fantastic for quickly putting a point across.'

Robert believes the H.P.A. 'will just assume that I will do the job until I say differently'.

The two hats Robert may be wearing during a polo match are quite different. As third man he will be keeping a close eye on how the two umpires are doing and how the game is progressing. 'Generally, for ninety-nine per cent of the time, the third man only decides between the umpires when they cannot agree on the nature of a play. All he would be saying if the necessity arises is, yes it was a foul or no it wasn't.'

During the one and a half hours of play Robert's duty as Chief Umpire ceases and after the match is over, he will go over to the two umpires to either tell them 'well done', or, 'look, we could have done this a bit better'. The third man however, would never go up to the umpires to comment on the way the game was umpired. Robert confesses: 'As soon as the match ends the third man is usually off to the bar!'

His newly acquired job of Chief Umpire is, however, more taxing. During the season Robert is

**Pick-up sticks and ball bags
– part of an umpire's tools**

in charge of putting together weekly meetings with the ten professional umpires employed by the H.P.A., during which they go over points of the week before. They study videos to see 'whether we are doing a good job, a reasonable job or a terrible job'.

All umpires have to pass a test and be approved by the stewards at the beginning of the polo season.

One of the main criteria for becoming a professional umpire is to have played the game at a certain level. The ten professionals are made up of a combination of players. There is Howard Hipwood who, in his heyday, held a nine-goal handicap and then there are others who played off three or four. Robert explains. 'What is important is that they have played, and we will obviously like to draw on players who played as high a goal polo as possible but the highest-goal player does not necessarily make the best umpire!' And, although Robert points out that having a good understanding of the rules is important, he stresses that having a feeling for the game is an absolute must.

'Sometimes a good umpire will let a minor foul go in the interest of a more flowing game and therefore apply the advantage rule. On other occasions, the umpire will blow the whistle and give a severe penalty because he saw a play which was potentially very dangerous.' The main purpose of umpiring must be to keep the game safe and most rules in polo are therefore based on this criterion.

Robert too was an accomplished polo player and has been seriously involved in polo since 1971. His biggest chance came at the age of eighteen when his future American father-in-law James Sharp - nicknamed Hap - asked him to spend a year playing polo with him in Argentina and England. 'I made a deal with my father that if he would let me go to Argentina for a year I would join the army.'

At the end of the 1971 season when Robert played for a low-goal team which won nineteen

Julian Appleby, another
member of the professional
umpires squad employed by
the Hurlingham Polo
Association.

Argentine polo player Dario
Musso on his way to his
umpire duties during the
2003 Deauville Gold Cup
tournament.

' I enjoy umpiring. It's
true that it can be tricky at
times, particularly as you
often have to umpire
matches involving friends
and colleagues. Games can
get quite heated at times,
and so it is really important
to remain cool and
objective, and to really
concentrate. An umpire can
make or break a match so I
take the role very seriously.
You have to be unbiased, be
able to concentrate and have
authority.'

matches, drew one and only lost one out of twenty-one, the time was ripe to strike another deal with his father!

'After Hap told Colonel Harper, secretary of the H.P.A. at the time, to look out for me, Colonel Harper called my father and suggested I join the Sharp organization. I told my father that I would do it for a year and then join the army. The truth is, however, I never managed to join the army. My brother did though. He bailed me out!'

Robert also remembers that aged thirteen he did not enjoy polo as much as he did later on. 'I did enjoy hitting a ball but horses didn't really interest me. They represented an awful lot of work for little enjoyment.'

The turning point came when Robert started acquiring an eye for the pretty New Zealand grooms his father used to employ. 'I started hanging around the stables much more and also found out that hitting a ball from a horse is a lot of fun after all.' Later on he also discovered that polo is a way of life. 'Polo gets hold of you and doesn't let go; like a pretty woman!'

Robert's highest handicap was six, and during the years of 1975 and 1976 he also played with his brother-in-law, Tommy Wayman, who became a ten-goal player. Together they won the King's Cup in Madrid when it was a twenty-five-goal tournament, and the Gold Cup in Sotogrande. He also made it to the final of the Gold Cup at Cowdray with Guy Wildenstein, a match the team sadly lost in extra time. Robert's fondest memory as a player is that polo

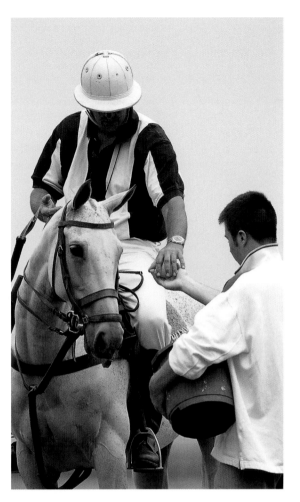

Juan José 'JJ' Diaz Alberdi stocking up on polo balls. Umpires carry spare balls in a leather ball bag attached to the saddle in front of the pommel. 'The idea is to keep the game flowing. So in case the ball goes flying over the boards we can replace it without losing too much time.'

opens doors. 'I can go to twelve countries in the world and know somebody there because of polo.'

He would, however, argue that polo is also a dangerous sport, especially at the lower level and, inevitably, Robert has the scars to prove it. 'All my injuries happened in the low-goal polo. Some of the worst incidents I have seen is when you have inexperienced players. At the higher level, polo might get rough but it is not as dangerous.'

His routine as a young man soon established itself: playing polo in Europe during the European season and living in Argentina for the rest of the year where he mostly played at his local polo club, which was none other than the outstanding Coronel Suárez. Robert also managed Hap's land, farming cattle and various crops, but breeding horses and playing polo were very much the predominant interests. The farm now belongs to Robert and his American wife, and he has the same way of life, with less emphasis on playing the game owing to the tight schedule of his current job.

Over the past twenty-five years Robert has seen the face of polo change considerably. Not only do players no longer come over to England just for an air ticket and somewhere to stay, but also the professional

umpires are connected to the third man via radio link, and since the radios have come down in size considerably Robert is a great advocate of their use. 'The radios keep the game moving. We don't want to waste time and have umpires riding from the farthest ends of the field to speak with the third man.' Robert feels that radios are fantastic for quickly putting a point across and recalls an anecdote that proves his point.

'It was during a match played by Black Bears.

One of the teams had scored and all the players, with the exception of patron Urs Schwarzenbach, left the field to change ponies. The umpire was about to throw in the ball with only one man on the field so he called me on the radio asking me whether he should go ahead? I told him yes, because the rule book says so, and Urs took the ball down to the goal by which time the defending team, who were changing ponies at that goal's end, realized what had happened in time to prevent Urs from scoring! It was the only time I have ever witnessed a player being outnumbered by the umpires.'

Another point that Robert wants to emphasize is that as Chief Umpire he would not want to see an umpire allow himself to get into an argument with one of the players.

'Of course players will be charged up during an important match, and as an umpire you might be a bit tolerant of that, but we don't want a player on the field talking to an umpire enough for the other team to think that by doing so that player might get an advantage out of the umpire. I therefore always encourage umpires to keep talking to a minimum.'

These points do get stressed in the weekly umpires' meetings and at the beginning of each tournament in the meetings Robert holds with the players.

'The meetings before the Queen's Cup are usually much better attended than the one before

Both parties have to realize that an important characteristic of an umpire is to strike a good balance between authority and true understanding.

Robert's job is a pleasant one yet one that also comes with its fair share of challenges.

the Gold Cup because most patrons will have seen how the season has developed and will use their own judgment as to whether they want to attend a second meeting or not.'

Robert has also had to go and speak to players individually. However, one of his main objectives is to avoid problems. He does not want to have to introduce incident report forms and is always in favour of sorting things out by keeping a good level of communication going. 'I also have a system by which players can call me and voice their concerns which might lead to going over a video together.'

'The nicest accomplishment is to get to the end of each year and to be able to say that there have been no major incidents on the field. The aim at the end of each match would be for the teams to have had played well and for the umpires to have gone unnoticed. So once the final of the Gold Cup has come along and I can say that there have not been any serious disciplinary matters, nobody got injured because of an incident on the polo field and, best of all, the players don't remember who umpired their matches, I would say we have had a successful season'

(Opposite and above) Goal judges between chukkas.

WHAT MAKES A TEN-GOAL PLAYER?

Paying tribute to one particular sportsman in a sport which is essentially a team sport can be quite a difficult affair. In polo, no matter how good a player happens to be, he is still primarily part of a team as opposed to competing as an individual. Furthermore, to participate in their chosen sport, polo players also partner other living beings, namely horses, animals with minds and personalities of their own.

Another slight complication is that a polo player can, for one tournament, have three team-mates who could very well be his opponents in another event. This is dictated by the fact that polo gets regulated on a handicap system.

Depending on their ability and success, each player is given a handicap ranging from minus two through to the highest accolade, ten.

Similarly, tournaments are also graded with the objective of making up a total handicap consisting of the combined handicaps of the four players forming a team. These tournaments are subdivided into low-, medium- and high-goal competitions. The purpose of applying a handicap system is to get teams of equal ability competing against each other. What this effectively means is that all teams competing in a particular tournament must add up to a total handicap of twenty-two goals. Finding the right combination of polo players to complete a team can

therefore become a bit of a challenge! However, a team that could only muster four players totalling a handicap of twenty-one can still compete. The lower-handicapped team would then start the match with an advantage of one goal in order to make up for the deficit in handicap.

To confuse you just a little more, there are of course exceptions to that rule. Some events, the Argentine Open being one of them, are classified as 'open' which means that teams don't necessarily have to add up to the same handicap when competing against each other. A team with the highest possible handicap of forty could on this occasion be playing against a team with a handicap of only thirty-five. Both teams would nonetheless begin the match on equal terms.

Taking all of the above into account, you will understand that I was able to narrow down my choice of player to whom to pay tribute by picking one who has already been given the highest rating and is playing off a ten-goal handicap. These ten-goal players would have not only shown amazing ability and skill, but would also have won a considerable number of high-goal tournaments throughout their playing career. There are, however, quite a few polo players currently playing off ten goals!

Adolfo hitting the ball on the turn during the 2003 semi-final Gold Cup match between Dubai and Hildon Sport.

Adolfo Cambiaso, playing for La Dolfina, just about to score in the semi-final of the 2003 Argentine Open in Palermo. Hard on his tail is Horacio Heguy, Indios Chapaleufu I.

'What makes Palermo more special is the crowd. Palermo is probably good for a player's ego. Playing here is part of my job but in addition to that I derive much of the same enjoyment from playing polo here as anywhere in the world.'

My aim in featuring just one ten-goal player was by no means to suggest that he might be the best player of all time, but merely to find out what lies behind a person who has devoted his life to a sport he loves and to find out what qualities he himself thinks he has that have helped him achieve the highest distinction.

One thing I had already found out while putting together my other three books, *Visions of Show Jumping*, *Visions of Eventing* and *Visions of Dressage*, was that success in all disciplines involving horses is founded on good horsemanship. Winning alone does not equal greatness in a sport that includes another living being. Whether it be a show jumper, event rider, dressage rider or polo player, they must all have a deep-rooted love for horses. All good competitors know that they must respect the animal in order for it to give its best.

This respect for the horses he is riding coupled with an almost mystical feeling for horses, will turn a good, skilful polo player into a great one.

The difference with polo, however, is that, not only do the players strive to 'click' with all the ponies they are riding during a match, they must also display a more-than-useful level of eye-to-ball coordination. In addition, polo is also a very physical contact sport; players are regularly seen riding each other off at tremendous speed. A polo player also has to be quick thinking, react fast, adapt rapidly to changing situations, and be able to translate tactics into action.

Players can usually be divided into two categories: some players prefer to take up the position of forward running and attacking, while for others the defensive play comes more naturally. But then there are those players who are good in any position. They are the players who have won tournaments playing in position one, two, three or even four, which is pretty remarkable to say the least.

One of these versatile players is the outstanding

Adolfo on his way to scoring a vital goal for Dubai in the team's 2003 Queen's Cup semi-final match against Azzurra.

Mexican horseman Carlos Gracida. He won the Argentine Open playing at one and four and the US Open playing at two and three.

Then there are those players who get awarded the highest handicap at a very young age and who manage to hold on to their ranking for a long time. The one name that stands out in that respect is that of Argentine polo star Adolfo Cambiaso. Adolfo is undoubtedly one of the sport's most outstanding players. His eye-to-ball coordination is second to none, his riding ability is remarkable and his mallet control unparalleled.

'I was so happy to have won because I thought that Azzurra was the best team around, even better then us. The match was like a final. Everything had gone against us that day. Ali had a broken finger and we were three goals down in the fifth chukka. Yet we won purely because we believed that we were going to win! When you think that you are going to lose, well, you do end up losing!'

Everybody involved in polo acknowledges Adolfo Cambiaso's ingenuity, a fact that led me towards taking a closer look at the Argentine who has been at the top of his sport since the age of fifteen, and to choosing him as the representative ten-goal player.

Adolfo Cambiaso

'For me, polo is fun!' Born on April 15th 1975 in Buenos Aires, Argentina, Adolfo Cambiaso has an extraordinary talent for the sport he absolutely loves. When you ask him what his talent consists of, you only get a shrug of the shoulders accompanied by a charming smile. 'Really, you have to ask other people because I don't know!' Perhaps he does not

Adolfo Cambiaso, enjoying a relaxing moment drinking *mate* **(a herbal tea).**

know because his playing is instinctive and inherent. He can only tell you that the first time he was exposed to polo was in his mother's womb and that the minute he was born he was probably already sitting on a polo pony! He played his first tournament at the age of eight and insists that he was much too young to analyse what polo would eventually mean to him.

One thing is certain though, winning represents a big part of it and Adolfo has done plenty of that! He became a professional polo player at fifteen and one year on got his first contract playing for Australian patron Kerry Packer and his Ellerston White team. At seventeen he became a ten-goal player in the USA and in England, the highest handicap a player can achieve. The Argentine Polo Association waited just another two years before they gave Adolfo this highest distinction in 1994. When asked if that had made him the youngest ever ten-goal player, he admits never to have thought about it!

Adolfo's early success meant that he never finished school. He was supposed to take his exams at the very time he was also picked to play the Argentine Open. He chose polo and, judging by the way he graces all major polo fields around the world, Adolfo made the right choice: 'I never look back on it. I was a terrible student anyway!'

Giving my initial question more thought, Adolfo says that he has been fortunate enough to have played with, and learned from, great players. 'I started with Ernesto Trotz, Gonzalo Pieres, Memo

Queen's Cup final, 2003.
Adolfo at full speed heading
towards the boards where
the ball seems to have taken
refuge for a split second. On
Cambiaso's tail is Sebastian
Dawnay. Adolfo is on
Pampita, his best horse in
England. She won Best
Playing Pony in the final.

'I like Pampita because I
saw her race and after the
race she was quiet whereas
all the other horses were
wound up. I bought her for
her temperament – she cost
$2000 – and played her the
next day. She was definitely
born to play polo; she has a
fantastic mouth, her
conformation is great and I
also thought that she would
make a great broodmare.'

(Right and opposite) Adolfo
is demonstrating a copybook
backhand on Matera, one of
Dubai's mares, during a
match against Cadenza.

Commenting on the shot
Adolfo agrees that it looks
like a good shot and that
the angle of his arm and the
mallet are in the perfect
position. His eyes are firmly
fixed on the ball, and Matera
is perfectly balanced and in
harmony with Adolfo. 'I don't
know how I do it. I have
never studied my shots.'

and Carlos Gracida and learned a lot by watching, talking, listening and playing.' Adolfo agrees that he must have taken the best bit from each one of them, especially as they all taught him different things, and he is quick to add, 'A good player is one who doesn't think he knows it all!' When he was young he played with practically everyone and emphasizes the importance of this. 'Every time you are on the field and every time you talk about polo you learn.' He does, after a while, admit to believing that he has talent but clarifies that talent alone is not enough.

Still wanting to get to the bottom of what makes Adolfo the brilliant player he is, I found myself changing tactics slightly by asking him what the game of polo is all about and what makes a good player?

'You need to understand the game and know how to get to the field well organized and how to put together a good team. If you play with bad horses, if you pick the wrong players, pick the wrong places to play at, it can damage your self-confidence.'

As stated, Adolfo's will and desire to win is boundless and, to realize that, the self-confidence, which seems to ooze from Adolfo, is a prerequisite.

Money is not his main motivation. In fact he often plays without getting paid. On the other hand Cambiaso feels very lucky to have a job for which he gets paid for doing something he absolutely loves. 'Today, I can honestly say that if I had to choose between playing a certain tournament and money, I would pick the tournament!'

Being a step ahead of the game is another of Adolfo's trademarks, one which he says comes with experience and playing as much as possible.

'I learn more about the game every day and hope to carry on learning. You don't only learn about what happens on the field but also about getting your ponies in shape and performing at their best for when it most counts.'

All the knowledge Adolfo has acquired over the years make him the player he is today and he believes that polo is not only about playing and scoring; it is also about the way you pick a horse and how you treat it.

Adolfo's passion is most certainly the horses. He loves breeding them and has up to 600 horses on his farm in Argentina. 'We have about 150 foals a year and I know every single one by name. I know its dam and which stallion it is by.' His passion is accompanied by his conviction that today the best way to be well mounted and to maintain his ten-goal handicap is to produce his own horses. 'The start of this process is the breeding of my own polo ponies.' All of his thoroughbred mares come from New Zealand, Australia and England. 'They are the best!' And the most important quality a polo pony must have for Adolfo is: 'A good mouth. The horse has to stop well and not run away. The rest is secondary.' Adding to that he simply points out, 'If a horse doesn't have a good mouth I won't play it!'

It is easy to recognize Adolfo on the polo field by his polo helmet showing the Argentine flag. The story behind this started in 2001 when a friend told

Adolfo that he probably wouldn't have the nerve to change his boring grey helmet for one with the design of a tiger on it. Little did his friend know him, because Adolfo did just that. He wore 'this ugly tiger image on his helmet and everybody knew him because of that.' Later Adolfo changed the image again. 'A year on I decided to change it for the Argentine flag because the country wasn't doing too well and in my own way I felt that by wearing the flag on my helmet I could support my country in my own small way!' It proved to be lucky; displaying the flag, Adolfo won the Argentine Open in Palermo that year.

Cambiaso feels that his best achievement to date, however, must have been winning every tournament he had entered in 1998. He also has fond memories of winning the Triple Crown, i.e. all three major tournaments in Argentina. Although he seems to be taking his achievements in his stride, Adolfo's wonderfully expressive eyes light up when he remembers having scored sixteen goals in a single match three times and sixty-seven goals in five matches. It is probably safe to say that Adolfo will hold onto this record for some years to come! Is it a record Adolfo perhaps wants to break himself? In his nonchalent way Adolfo simply replies, 'No, no these goals just

Adolfo's trademark. 'I felt like putting the Argentine flag on my helmet because the country wasn't doing so well and, by wearing the flag on my helmet, I felt that I could support my country in my own small way!"

happened and if you ever think about that you wouldn't score a single goal.'

In England, when playing for Dubai, Adolfo usually plays at number three and acts as the playmaker for the team. In Argentina however, Adolfo likes playing at one, which he considers being the most difficult position to be playing from nowadays.

'Things have changed in polo. you don't just stay up front as number one. You have to go back and go forward again. In football you would call that position "*libero*". However, to make the most of playing as a *libero* your team-mates have to be very strong in their roles as number two, number three and at the back. If this is the case, it's great because then the number one can do whatever he wants. And, I like that!'

For that perfect play, as well as for when he plays in England, Adolfo's partner in crime is his best friend and brother-in-law Bartolome 'Lolo' Castagnola. The two grew up in the game together from when they were both zero-handicap players. Neither of them comes from a big polo-playing family which is something that drew them closer.

'I was on my own and so was Lolo and we just happened to grow into a couple which in polo terms becomes very important. Being by yourself, won't get you anywhere in polo! We needed each other then and still do now. We got to the top by discussing things and by thinking of ways to improve. Always together.'

In 22 to 26-goal polo things are slightly different

Adolfo Cambiaso moving towards goal in Dubai's first league match of the 2004 Queen's Cup tournament. The newly formed team of Graff Capital with patron Markus Graff, brothers Pablo and Matias MacDonough and Mark Tomlinson gave Dubai a run for their money.

Ali Saeed Albwardi's team won thanks to Adolfo's goal in the very last seconds of the match when riding Edna, a mare Adolfo bought from Ellerston when she was still a bit green. 'She is fantastic, like a machine! She has played everywhere: in the United States, in Argentina, in Spain, in England.'

though. Here Adolfo plays at three and Lolo at two because the emphasis is put on creating a strong and tough midfield. 'The game is more or less won in the midfield and you play easy with the number one and the back.'

Regardless of which tournament they play in, their goal is to win. Yet Adolfo is quick to add that if he does lose he is never afraid of losing his job because a patron has to realize that polo is a team sport.

'It is important to show a patron who you are and for the patron to understand that whether the team wins or loses you do it as a team because you all pull together. A team's destiny does not depend on one player alone or the umpire.'

In Ali Albwardy, patron of Dubai, Adolfo seems to have found the perfect man: understanding, encouraging, compassionate, passionate about horses and the game, coupled with a huge desire to win, the two seem to be made for each other. Neither of them likes to be in the limelight and they both enjoy being round horses and their team members either drinking *mate* (herbal tea) or having an *asado* (barbecue) more than socializing at big functions. Both men dote on their families; so far Adolfo has one daugher and Ali two sons. 'More than anything', both will tell you, 'we are friends'. And they could talk polo and horses until the cows come home.

Adolfo also likes spending time with his father, a three-times South American surfing champion. Every year the two take off together and Adolfo surfs and doesn't touch a polo ball for a month. He claims surfing to be his second-best sport. According to others, Adolfo is, however, also excellent at tennis, golf, skiing and snow boarding but, again, Adolfo is modest and only gives away that he is good enough at these sports 'to enjoy them and have fun'. And we all know what impact Adolfo can have on a sport when he is merely having fun!

So, how can one best describe the super and multi-talented Adolfo Cambiaso? In his own words he considers himself an easy-going, very quiet person and 'someone who likes to give a lot'. Yet, he is also someone who will be put in a bad mood when things don't go as he expects them to. 'When I put something in my mind, it has to happen and I usually give myself a three-year plan.'

Having won the Argentine Open in Palermo on four occasions, 1994, 1997, 1998 and 2002, with two different teams, Adolfo reveals that winning this particular event is no longer a burning desire and that he now needs time to think about and plan something new that he really wants to achieve.

Perhaps I should return to Adolfo's suggestion that I should 'ask other people' about what makes him stand out from his team-mates and fellow competitors. The following quotes reveal how other people in polo see Adolfo.

'Adolfo is a very simple man. His pleasure is coming down to the stables, seeing the horses, drinking mate *and talking to the grooms.'*
Ali Albwardy, patron of Dubai

'Adolfo is one with the horse. He is the horse. They work together. You never see him lose his temper with a horse and you never see him flustered by a horse. Everything he does on the field just flows. Adolfo defies the law of gravity. He gets to balls that no one else can reach. He is a natural. A truly accomplished sportsman.'

Pete McCormack, agent for La Dolfina

'Adolfo's reactions and thought processes are quicker than everybody else's. He goes to the ball and does things with it that others wouldn't entertain doing! It is not so much that other players wouldn't be able to do it. It just never enters their minds.'

Robert Thame, polo manager to Ali Albwardy

'Adolfo is the best polo player by far. But he is not the best rider. I don't think he could do well at dressage or show jumping! He and I like exactly the same type of horse. He likes a good mouth in a horse.'

Carlos Gracida

'Adolfo is a complete freak! How he gets his horses to run and make them do what he wants to do is amazing. He is great to watch. It would be an experience to play with him on a team. You wouldn't go to the polo ground with much pressure because you would just know that you would have a good chance of winning!'

Luke Tomlinson

Adolfo in a familiar position of reaching almost for the impossible just ahead of Gonzalito Pieres during the match against Ellerstina in the 2003 Argentine Open. Adolfo teamed up with Lolo Castagnola and the Merlos brothers, Sebastian and Pite, to play as La Dolfina.

'Initially Lolo and I were going to play for Ellerstina with Gonzalito but then things changed and we ended up playing in that formation. In the Argentine Open you usually end up playing with players you are good friends with or you are related to. Lolo and I are good friends with Sebastian and he wanted to play with his brother Pite.'

La Dolfina reached the final when they were beaten by La Aguada, the four Novillo-Astrada brothers' team.

'It is always daunting playing Adolfo because he is a bit of a freak. He has taken polo to another level and really he is an eleven- or even twelve-goal player.'
Mark Tomlinson

'Adolfo is very quick to read a situation. He is very aware of distance and position, and he has an amazing eye to control the ball. Actually he has an incredible arrogance on the field which in his case is not offensive. He is arrogant in as far as he will take the ball without really minding if any one of his team-mates touches the ball. He will just go ahead and score! Anybody else, especially English players, would be embarrassed because we have not been brought up that way; in the old days if you turned the ball once it was considered bad polo. However, Adolfo is, in a word, amazing!'
Howard Hipwood

'I really don't know what makes Cambiaso special but, by the same token, I couldn't tell you what makes Schumacher special. The difference between the two is that Michael actually works a lot at his skills. I have known Adolfo over fifteen years and I have certainly never seen him work at his skills. So, I don't know where and when he learned to play how he does. It must be in his genes. To sum him up, he is a twelve-goal player.'
Urs Schwarzenbach

'Cambiaso is a crack! You never know what he is about to do next. Playing against him is extremely difficult. He always has a new trick up his sleeve. I have played against him four times and only won once!'
Juan Martin Nero

'I would say Adolfo has exactly what I don't have: amazing ability on the ball and a lot of strength. He can win any ride-off, he can hit the ball a hundred yards if he needs to, or tap the ball in the air going flat out!'
Pepe Araya

'Cambiaso is an extraterrestrial; amazing; from another planet! For me, he is the best player. I find him very quiet. He is very much into his own group. When playing against him I find that he is very focused and concentrates on his game.'
Pelon Stirling

'Adolfo is the best player in the world. He is an absolute natural. Comparing abilities I would say he is the Maradona of polo. He can do in ten minutes what takes me two hours. If I have to work my horses, he sends his out in the field and they go just as well as mine! Also, he is like a brother.'
Lolo Castagnola, team-mate and brother-in-law

Adolfo Cambiaso transfixes the ball and is about to take a swing at it in midair during the 2004 Veuve Cliquot semi-final match between Dubai and Graff Capital.

Gillian Johnston has been
playing polo since 1995 and
plays 'pretty much full time'.

'I am hooked on polo,
mainly because I just love
horses. I used to ride rodeo
and show jump but I got
bored with them because
there was just so much
hanging around.'

When competing in
England Gillian is based at
her farm in the village of
Graffham, just a ten-minute
drive from Cowdray Polo
Club. In this photo, Gillian is
on Destineda in the semi-
final of the 2003 Gold Cup.

'Destineda is a mare from
Argentina. She was new to
me that season and
developed into one of my
best horses. She is not the
fastest horse, but is very
handy and has a soft mouth.'

POLO IN ACTION

Adolfo Cambiaso on the attack during the quarter-final match against Les Lions, in the Veuve Cliquot Gold Cup, Cowdray 2004. Tariq Albwardi is keeping a close eye on things.

Adolfo Cambiaso is trying to catch up with Nina Vestey and hook her during the semi-final of the 2003 Veuve Cliquot Gold Cup.

Nina the youngest of three polo-playing children was six years old when she started playing polo with the Cotswold Pony Club. 'Dad threw us all on a pony pretty much at the same time.' Nina used to event as well as play polo and it was only at the age of seventeen that polo finally took over from eventing because she had had bad luck with her eventing horses.

'When going into the semi-final match against Dubai we didn't think we stood a chance. I found that whenever I was within three yards of the two ten-goalers, Adolfo or Lolo, I was incredibly nervous! When I won the ball and they were anywhere near me I thought that I would never be able to keep the ball without them snatching it from me. In this sequence I am on my best horse, Treacle. She is incredibly fast and I thought that I might just outrun Adolfo but he caught me in the end. It is nice to know that Cambiaso feels I am a valuable enough player for him to make such an effort to hurt me. Playing next to people of his calibre is amazing. It was awe-inspiring because I was right beside them and saw what they are capable of doing!'

(Opposite) Nacho Gonzales playing for Black Cats in a 2003 Queen's Cup league match against Dubai, at Dubai's home ground in Holyport.

'You have a lot of respect when you are playing against Dubai because they have two great players in Adolfo Cambiaso and Lolo Castagnola. Adolfo is simply the best player right now. Playing against him, one should never attempt to upset him. Because if you do, he will tell you so by scoring four goals in a flash! Adolfo plays on a different level and he can turn it on whenever he wants to.'

Nacho, born to an Argentine father and English mother, is based at the Royal Berkshire Polo Club. Like all professional polo players, Nacho travels extensively once the English polo season is over. His finest achievement came in 1993 when he won the Gold Cup with team-mates Piki Alberdi and Gabriel Donoso for Alcatel.

Pablo Mora Figueroa keeping the ball in play and directing it towards goal during a match between his team, Santa Maria-Graffham, and Ciguiñuelas-John Smith, Sotogrande 2004.

Pablo and his brother Ramón run and own the Santa Maria Polo Club. Enrique Zobel a great friend of the brothers' father was, however, the pioneer of Sotogrande and created the first fields in 1967. Sadly Enrique passed away in 2004. The Gold Cup tournament was first held in 1968.

The Mora family are main shareholders of the Coca Cola bottling business for Southern Spain. Pablo loves being a businessman and it also means that he can earn enough money to be able to play polo, not only as a hobby but also competitively. 'I love the sport and spend every extra penny I have on polo! I also spend every single free minute I have around polo! I am happy because I have won the Gold Cup six times and the Silver Cup nine times.'

Due to his business commitment, Pablo only plays in Spain. Besides, living in Southern Spain means that Pablo is blessed with being able to play polo every weekend throughout the entire year. 'We are very comfortable here. We have good horses and a lot of good players come to play in our tournaments.'

David 'Pelon' Stirling in the red
shirt playing for Diablos
running neck and neck with
Milo Fernandez-Araujo, Loro
Piana-Terranova. Both teams
are almost mirroring each
other in a match during the
Sotogrande Gold Cup
tournament.

Uruguayan Pelon started
playing polo in Sotogrande at
the age of sixteen. Because his
father ran the Sotogrande Polo
Club until 2002, Pelon has lived
there all his life.

'We have prestigious
tournaments here in
Sotogrande. Maybe they are not
as prestigious as the big
tournaments in England but our
Gold Cup is at the same level as
the Deauville Gold Cup, which is
played at the same time.'

Together with Gonzalito
Pieres, Pelon won the sixteen-
goal Ellerston Challenge Cup for
Ellerston in Ellerston, March
2004.

Now that Pelon has finished
his studies in marketing
management and leisure
planning he wants to
concentrate even more on polo.

'I will go to Argentina more
in the hope of staying there for
the season. I have always
wanted to be a professional
polo player and my goal is to
get the chance to play the
Argentine Open. If you are not
Argentine it becomes less
achievable, yet nothing is
impossible if you want it badly
enough!'

British patron Tony Pidgley out in front in the 2004 subsidiary semi-final of the Queen's Cup. A match his team, Cadenza, won, beating Dubai. Tony has been involved in polo since 1992. A trademark of his team is to proudly fly the British flag!

'There are a lot of foreign teams competing but there were no English high-goal patrons, and so I decided to get into high goal in 2003. I play a lot of snow polo; together with Jack Kidd I won in Kitzbühl, Aspen and the first ever polo tournament played in Moscow. If you ask me for my goals, I'd like to win the Queen's Cup and the Gold Cup!'

(Opposite) During the 2003 season, Pablo Spinacci played for Ladyswood in England and in Deauville. This picture was taken at Cirencester Polo Club in a match against Black Bears which Ladyswood won in overtime.

Pablo's biggest achievement to date is winning the Palm Beach Silver Cup twenty-goal tournament in Florida.

Agustin Garcia-Grossi in full
swing during the semi-final
match against Loro Piana-
Settiponti.

Agustin had never
teamed up with Marcos di
Paola before the Gold Cup
tournament and described
his team-mate and
playmaker as a great player.
'Marcos organized the team
very well.'

Andrea Vianini and Eduardo Novillo-Astrada battling for the ball in a match for the 2003 Warwickshire Cup played at the Cirencester Polo Club.

What excites Andrea most about polo is 'when the horse you are riding is going really well and you are scoring a great goal'.

'Primarily I play polo because I love horses. I would go as far as saying that I care more about the horses than the players on the field. I don't mean this in a negative way, but when it comes to polo I don't really mind who I am playing against. I never think of the opposition. I turn up and play against whoever.'

Andrea Vianini, playing for Ladyswood, about to hit a backhander almost on the turn during a match for the 2003 Warwickshire Cup against Foxcote.

'I am on my lovely nine-year-old gelding Cacho, saving the ball from crossing the goal line.'

Andrea enjoys playing polo in England. He has won a lot of fifteen-goal tournaments and the Challenge Cup at Cowdray two years in a row.

'I play well here. It must be the weather. I like playing in the mud!'

Andrea Vianini showing his love for speed!

Andrea started playing polo as a child. He first came over to England in 1987 at the age of nineteen. In 1990 he stopped playing polo altogether for three years and raced formula three cars.

'I love speed. My father raced in formula three, two and one. Sadly he had a car accident at twenty-seven that paralysed him. I was racing well in South America but Europe is where the money is. The reason I stopped is because I had spent all the money I had made in polo. So I had to go back to it to make money again! Also, I love horses. I live on a farm and playing polo is what I do best. My craziness and love for speed comes from my paternal genes. My mother is the polo girl! A perfect combination!'

Alejandro Vial and Adam Tolhurst in a league match between Chile and Australia for the 2004 Federation of International Polo World Championships, Chantilly.

Before travelling to France to represent his country, Alejandro had already been a member of the victorious Chilean team – with brothers Gabriel and José Donoso and Jaime Huidobro – that claimed this year's Coronation Cup, having beaten England.

Adam and the Australian team qualified for the World Championships by coming first, ahead of Pakistan, in the Australasian Zone. Adam, from New South Wales, had also already represented his country in the match between Young Australia and Young England, which England won in November 2003. Adam started playing polo thanks to the influence of his father, a keen player himself.

'For me polo is linked with the enjoyment of hitting the ball, and, once you have reached a certain stage, it's a sport where there is no limit; you just keep on improving and improving. The better I became the more enjoyment I got out of it. I'll keep playing for a long time and, hopefully, I'll keep improving. Playing here was a great honour. To come and play for my country has been an amazing experience. We are a bit disappointed with our results but apart from that it has been a great tournament and a great learning curve.'

On the day, Chile won 16–5.

(Opposite) James Beim and Martin Jose Gastaldi during the final of the 2003 European Championship held at Dallas Buston. By beating Italy, England qualified for the 2004 World Championship in Chantilly, France.

'Playing the European Championships was great fun. We were put under a bit of pressure by a lot of people including the H.P.A. They all expected us to win. We were the favourites especially as we were playing at home. We had lost to Italy in a league match but that didn't really matter because we had already qualified for the semi-final. However, losing shook us up and Italy had possibly become the favourite on finals day. I think we shocked Italy by going 4–nil up in the first chukka. They never really recovered and we kept well to our team plan.'

Pepe Heguy playing for Labegorce during the 2003 Gold Cup quarter-final against Oakland Park.

Pepe, short for Alberto, has played fifteen seasons in England. He started to play polo at the age of eight yet only became a professional at twenty-three because first he wanted to finish his degree in agriculture. Pepe has won the Queen's Cup twice: once with Labegorce and once with Ellerston. He has also won the Argentine Open three times.

'I am on my favourite mare, Comadreja. I have played her a lot over the last two years. The brother of the Sultan of Brunei used to play her. Bautista brought her over from Argentina. I kept her with Labegorce for the 2002 and 2003 seasons. Now I will take her to play in Italy.'

Pepe Heguy on the ball moving towards the goal during the 2003
Gold Cup quarter-final match in which Labegorce beat Oakland Park.

'It was a really difficult match to win. Pablo MacDonough and
Marcos di Paola played really well. Pablo replaced Gonzalito Pieres
who had injured his hand earlier in the season.

'What I am best at in polo is handling the speed and being a
good team player. Polo is really a big part of my life. It is my work
but mostly I do it because I enjoy it. Outside Argentina I play as a
professional but back home I play purely for fun with my friends. If I
wasn't playing polo I would just live on my farm with my family. I
would always have horses because they are my life.'

English polo player James Beim turned professional at the age of eighteen when he was first asked to play for Ellerston. James had a lot of success playing for the 'White team' in 1998, 1999 and 2000. After that he travelled to Australia and Argentina during the European winter months.

'I have been based at Ellerston over the winter months since 2000. I love it there. It's like my second home. I know everybody there; they are either father figures or best mates! Playing for Ellerston is amazing. You are always mounted really well. But this luxury doesn't come without pressure because you are always expected to win! Polo is my life and I have to pinch myself sometimes to believe how lucky I am that I do not have to sit at a desk.'

American patron Gillian Johnston on her nine-year-old homebred mare Sealy during the 2003 Gold Cup semi-final. Although getting off to a good start, Gillian's team, Graffham, with players Miguel Novillo-Astrada, Tommy Llorente and Tom Morley, lost to Labegorce.

'Sealy is my best mare. I have been playing her in high goal since she was four. I normally don't start my horses in high goal that young but she is a natural! She is very handy, consistent and very reliable. The match was actually going our way in the first half. We got ahead and then Labegorce came back. Basically we lost our momentum, which was a real shame.'

Nina Vestey, Hildon Sport,
and Pepe Heguy, Labegorce,
during the 2003 Veuve
Cliquot Gold Cup final.

Nina is riding Jack, a
New Zealand thoroughbred.
'I got him from John Paul
Clarkin's father. Jack is
fantastic, incredibly tough
and very good in ride-offs! I
played him for two chukkas
throughout the entire Gold
Cup tournament. He is
incredibly fast, nimble and
handy. I just adore him!'

Hildon Sport had already
beaten Labegorce in a
league match and felt very
confident of being able to
win the final too. When they
actually won, Nina's parents
were so thrilled that one of
their children was repeating
family history.

'My parents have been so
supportive throughout. They
come and watch every single
game I play, whether it's a
two-goal match or twenty-
two!'

Pepe's verdict on the
match was: 'Our horses were
"dead" so it made winning
the Gold Cup on that day
pretty impossible!'

Nina Vestey on Palito, just ahead of Adrian Kirby during the 2003
Queen's Cup tournament.

'I don't play Palito very often. He is a naughty little gelding!
Very sweet but he is not in my top string, which I discovered
during the Queen's Cup. This is also why I started doubling-up
Jack in the Gold Cup. Palito is a lovely horse to have as a spare
but he doesn't quite have the edge of my other horses.'

Nina Vestey on Fugitiva
coming off the field and
making her way to the pony
lines at the end of a chukka.

'In those moments I
usually reflect on how the
game has been going so far
and whether the team is
doing the right thing. You are
also thinking, "OK, right, next
chukka". I tell myself to
concentrate and to mark my
man. I try to refocus. I also
already know which horse I
will be getting on.'

Alejandro 'Piki' Diaz Alberdi hasn't missed playing the English
polo season since 1989. Since 1991 Piki has been playing off a
ten-goal handicap. He has won the Gold Cup twice: with Alcatel in
1993 and with Pomery in 1999. He got to the Queen's Cup final
three times but has thus far not won it.

During the 2004 season Piki teamed up with Bautista Heguy
and English player Ryan Pemble for Polish patron Marek Dochnal
and the Larchmont polo team. Piki sees playing for a patron who
has only just come into the sport as a big challenge.

'Marek came to me telling me that he wanted to play polo. I
want to make him the best player he can possibly be. This will
take time and realistically can't happen overnight. Marek is aware
of that. It is a process and I don't want Marek to win without
learning. Of course I want him to win too but Marek is young,
time is on his side and with it comes the potential for winning
lots of tournaments.'

In their first season in English high goal, Larchmont reached
the semi-final stages of both the Queen's Cup and the Gold Cup.

Piki Alberdi playing for Larchmont against Maybach during the 2004 St. Moritz tournament which is traditionally held in January and played on the frozen lake.

'We had only decided to play in St. Moritz a couple of weeks before the tournament. Marek had only just began to play polo in November 2003. He had a bet going that he would be playing in St. Moritz. I encouraged him to come to Argentina to practise. I told him that I would decide if he was up to it a week before the tournament. He worked hard and we played and we won!

'The horses get used to the snow quite easily. The main difference is the ball. It can fly anywhere because it is filled with air. So you end up hitting the ball in midair quite a lot. Because the ball is considerably larger than a normal polo ball, it makes getting to your opponent difficult. The trick is to try to open up the field and to be patient, then you are sure to score goals.'

Juan José Branne has played in St. Moritz four times but 2004 was the first time he played for Maybach.

'St. Moritz is a really nice tournament. I like playing on snow yet it is very different from playing on grass. I think it's a good show for the spectators. I do prefer playing on grass, it's what I am used to, besides, polo has its origins on grass!'

Italian patron Alfio Marchini making sure he keeps Marcos di Paola off the ball in the Sotogrande Gold Cup 2004. Alfio started playing polo and competing in 2002.

'Polo is a passion I developed quite easily. I first played in Sotogrande during the Easter tournament in 2003 and won it. This year I decided to enter two teams because there are a lot of players I like and they are like my younger brothers! Juan Martin and Gonzalito are not only really nice guys they are great sportsmen.

'I like playing and I am not the type of patron who wants to hold the big cups. I want to learn and I want to play. I love horses and I give 100 per cent when I am on the field. If we win, well that's great, and if we don't we just have to play better next time. Also, I see polo as a way to clear my mind of all my business worries. When I sit on a horse and play polo I forget everything else.'

Marcos di Paola hitting an under-the-neck shot in the quarter-final of the 2003 Queen's Cup.

'It's best never to think too much about the under-the-neck or any other shot the moment you are hitting it. The most important thing is to keep your eye on the ball. Years of experience playing all the various shots does also help. You just have to try to keep your concentration that's all. It's like in any other ball game, be it tennis or golf. The key is to keep focusing on the ball. In polo everything happens so fast of course and if you think about how best to execute a particular shot, it's already too late. After years of practice it all develops into a routine action. The most difficult shot is probably the under-the-neck shot on the nearside, especially when you are travelling at speed!'

Marcos rates his two wins in the Cámara de Deputados, 1998 and 2003, as his best successes.

Milo Fernandez-Araujo and
Mark Tomlinson playing in
the quarter-final of the
2004 Queen's Cup. On that
day Milo, who was being
marked very closely by
Mark, lost the match he was
playing for Loro Piana
against Graff Capital.

'We went into the match
thinking that we could win
it and were already thinking
who we were going to meet
in the semi-final. Yet
everything went wrong! We
couldn't hit the ball and we
truly underestimated our
opponents. Also, there was a
critical play towards the
end of the match. The play
indicated a foul which
would have given us the
chance to win the match
but the foul wasn't given.
Then there was a corner for
us and, again, the umpires
didn't give it, although the
other team admitted to it. I
got very upset because the
umpires didn't even listen
to what the other team was
saying! In a case like that
one really has to try and
block it out of one's mind
as quickly as possible but
it's very difficult.'

Milo Fernandez-Araujo managed to shake off Scapa patron Michael Redding.

'I really enjoy playing in Sotogrande. I like the people and the food is great! I won the Gold Cup in 2002 and the Silver Cup in 1988.'

This is not all Milo has won over the years! He is also a double winner of the Argentine Open: 1999 and 2000.

(Right and opposite) Ernesto Trotz during the 2003 Deauville Gold Cup tournament which he, Dario Musso, Mark Tomlinson and the Pailloncy brothers won for the HB team. Like most Argentine polo players Ernesto started riding at a very young age on his family's farm; in his case, at the age of three.

'My father was in the army and I always travelled with him which opened the door to polo for me.' Ernesto already had a one-goal handicap at fourteen. He became a professional in 1980 and won the Argentine Open six times. Deauville is not a bad playing ground for him either; he had his seventh Gold Cup win there in 2003.

Argentine player Ernesto Trotz (together with Gonzalo and Alfonso Pieres)
belongs to the first generation of players who decided to make a career out of
playing polo. Although he started to study, Ernesto didn't finish university
because he soon realized that playing polo was more fun than sitting in a
classroom.

'I started travelling. I was already a seven-goal player at the age of twenty-
one. So, I went to Florida, and there I won the US Open three times.

In 2004 Ernesto played the Gold Cup tournament for Max Gottschalk's team,
Les Lions.

'Oh look at that, I am passing Cambiaso! This is a great picture, my groom
will be very happy to see this! What happened was this: I first got passed Matt
Lodder, hit the ball well and then saw Cambiaso. I didn't know what would
happen so I sent my mare forward and she passed him. It was all down to her,
nothing to do with me! I bred her and love her! She is a really fabulous mare!
During that match she was certainly my best horse. It was a great match. I was
a bit scared before the match because Dubai had won their previous match by
more than ten goals. However, Les Lions played really well that day and
although we didn't manage to win we all felt good about the way we played.'

(Left and opposite) Tommy Fernandez-Llorente can almost be crowned the 'King of Sotogrande'. He has won the Gold Cup five times and the Silver Cup ten times. He became a professional polo player at the age of twenty-two. Like so many Argentine players, he too did not quite finish his studies as, again, polo was just so much more fun!

'I had two great opportunities to play: one to play in England for three months and the other to play in Spain. I just couldn't refuse! I only had one year left before graduating as a law student but, to tell you the truth, I have no regrets.'

**Spot the ball. It is there! The
player is Alejandro Muzzio and
the match is the final of the
2004 Sotogrande Gold Cup,
which uncharacteristically was
played in thick fog.**

Santiago Toccalino and
Nacho Domecq during the
2004 Gold Cup final,
Sotogrande.

Tommy Fernandez-Llorente played the
2003 English season for Gillian
Johnston's team, Graffham. Here he is
on Vasca, one of his best horses.

   'Vasca belongs to Pablo Mora
Figueroa, my patron in Sotogrande. He
gives me the horses and lets me take
them to England too. We are great
friends and have been together for
some twenty years.'

Agustin Garcia-Grossi teamed up with Marcos di Paola and Santiago Toccalino to play in Michael Redding's team, Scapa, during the 2004 Sotogrande Gold Cup tournament. Together they reached the final where foggy weather conditions added another dimension to the match against the eventual winners, Tradition.

Argentine Agustin, who is Italian on his mother's side, has been a professional polo player since 1998. After the Argentine polo season, he spends most of his time playing in Italy where he keeps a string of horses. At home his family have a farm where he enjoys breeding horses.

January 2004 was the first time Chilean polo player Jaime Huidobro had played in St. Moritz.

'I thought playing on the frozen lake was going to be quite a show but it was really very competitive! You need to play very good polo in order to win. It has its similarities with grass polo but you really cannot afford to make any mistakes because there is hardly any time to recover. Hitting the ball straight does represent some difficulty because the ball is full of air and the wind can carry it away from the direction you intended it to go in. Tapping the ball and hitting backhanders are almost the same as with a normal ball. On snow the game is slower but rougher: very physical and fast on the short plays which means you are better off getting rid of the ball quickly so that the other team doesn't take the ball from you. Then there is the cold weather; there is nothing you can really do to protect yourself against the cold. You just try to get warm during the first chukka. All in all it's a lot of fun, particularly as the tournament is so well organized. I would love to play there again.'

Jaime Huidobro, FCT, and JP Clarkin, Foxcote Red, during the 2003 Warwickshire Cup final. FCT won. Jaime talks about the team.

'Winning one of the high-goal tournaments in England is aways a great pleasure, especially when playing with friends. I played very well with Henry Brett two years ago. We reached the semi-final of the Queen's Cup which proves that we have a good understanding. Playing with Rookie and FCT patron Roger Carlsson was good too. We went on to reach the quarter-finals of the Gold Cup that year when we got beaten by Hildon Sport, the eventual Gold Cup winners, who caught us on a bad day.'

Jaime doesn't spend much time in his native Chile, but spends almost five months playing in England and three playing in St. Tropez.

'I also go to Argentina to improve. Polo is my passion. I could never tire of the game. Nothing can be better than having a passion for the job one does!'

English player Jack Kidd on Inkle, an English thoroughbred bred by Claire Tomlinson, during the 2004 St. Moritz final. Jack played for Marek Dochnal's team Larchmont.

'Playing polo in St. Moritz has been an amazing experience. It was my fourth attempt to win the tournament and this time I did! St. Moritz is a wonderful experience to take your top string to. As far as playing on snow goes, it has been an amazing year for me. I played in Moscow, Russia, Kitzbühel in Austria, Aspen in the US, and in St.Moritz, and I won all four snow championships! So now I have decided to stop snow polo and see whether I can become good on grass! Playing on snow suits my polo though, because it's more about aggression and physical contact. It's similar to the arena polo we play here in England – I went to eight goal in arena polo in America. It is definitely my forte, together with snow polo.'

Talandracas patron Edouard Carmignac about to score a goal during the 2004 Gold Cup tournament.

Edouard was born in Paris but when he was five he followed his parents to South America where he started riding. 'Playing polo was always a childhood dream. When I was five years old our house gave onto the grounds of the polo club in Lima, Peru, where I was raised. Coming home from school I saw these centaurs on their horses and I thought of being one of them when I grew up!'

He moved back to France when he was twelve. 'At thirty-five I could afford to start having a few horses and built up from there.' Edouard first entered his team, Talandracas, for the Veuve Cliquot Gold Cup in 2003. 'I have played a lot in France and Spain where I have won the Gold Cups in Deauville, 2002, and in Sotogrande, 2001. My aim now is to win the English Gold Cup and to have some fun while trying! I always like to win but primarily I enjoy playing polo! For me polo is a passion with which one can get the feeling of becoming a perfect part of a team. Of course scoring is fun! Polo keeps me fit, on my toes and young; what more can one ask!'

Andrew Hine, riding Silkwood, on the attack during the 2003 Coronation Cup when England played and beat Mexico.

'Silkwood was fifteen in 2003. I got her in Australia and sold her to the Sultan of Brunei. Bautista Heguy played her a lot when he was playing for Brunei. She nearly always got two chukkas in the big games. She is very handy, has a big heart and is great to hit off. I bought her back from Brunei when they sold all their horses five years ago. I have retired her now. It was time to put her in foal.'

Andrew spends half the year in Australia and the other in England. 'I have a farm in Australia and love it there! I love England too but for seven months of the year you can't play polo here which means you can't make money. I found spending the winter months away from England much more productive.'

Andrew sees his future in polo moving into the coaching side of it. 'Big teams are starting to recognize the benefits of having a very good coach and are starting to pay them accordingly too. To have someone on the side is very helpful. Someone who can see what is happening and can make tactical changes. I think having someone who is a team coordinator and horse manager and coach is the future of the sport and I'd love to be doing that.'

Emma Tomlinson's fascination
for polo is fuelled by her
determination to get better
and her love for horses.
'Horses are amazing athletes.
I love breeding horses and
bringing them on. Getting
them on to high-goal polo is
quite special.'

In her first season in high-
goal polo Emma teamed up
with Satnam Dhillon, Pepe
Araya and Santiago
Gaztambide to play the 2004
Veuve Cliquot Gold Cup
tournament. In the quarter-
final, playing for Beaufort,
Emma met her brother Mark
who was playing for Graff
Capital.

'The match against Graff
Capital was a good match. We
had a few very good chances
towards the end of the match
and I think we should have
won! In the sixth chukka we
missed a thirty-yarder, then a
shot in front of goal, about
ten or fifteen yards out, that
we didn't convert. All this in
the last minute of regular
time. So we should have been
up but we weren't! And then
it went into a seventh chukka
which can be anybody's and it
wasn't ours!

'The difference between
medium and high goal is the
speed and also it's played
much more cleanly. It's not as
scrappy and much more
enjoyable! I love the game
but more than that I love
experiencing the horses I have
produced playing well
underneath me and giving
their all. That is exhilarating!'

Stefano Marsaglia, patron of Azzurra, in a league match for the Queen's Cup when his team played Broncos. (Queen's Cup league matches often get assigned to other grounds. This one was played in Cowdray.) Here Stefano is battling it out with Clare Milford-Haven who replaced her husband, George, at number one for the day.

'Clare is a good friend but you have to forget that you are playing against a woman because on the polo field women are just as tough as men! You don't think about it and you do what needs to be done! I enjoy polo a lot. I like the pace that goes with it and the fact that it is a competitive game. I get quite excited, especially when I score because I don't score very often!'

Mark Tomlinson on his gelding Chico during the 2003 Veuve Cliquot Gold Cup final against Labegorce.

Mark, brother Luke and friends Nina Vestey and John Paul Clarkin teamed up for Hildon Sport during the 2003 English high-goal season. Although the team didn't start the season too well and needed the Queen's Cup tournament to even out things, they showed resilience, determination, self-belief and flair by winning the Gold Cup.

'When I get to the final stages of a tournament, I start playing only my best three, four horses. Chico is one of those that I start doubling up. If a horse is well looked after and is feeling well it can play two chukkas. You couldn't do it all season but for two or three matches you can. Chico is just the size I like. He is very agile and has a huge heart. I prefer geldings to mares; I feel that they have more staying power in them. A mare might tell you where to go after four or five minutes play!'

Gonzalito Pieres playing for Loro Piana-Setteponti in full stretch during the 2004 Sotogrande Gold Cup semi-final. Santiago Toccalino, Scapa, is trying to interfere. Scapa won this match yet lost the final to Tradition.

Gonzalito was born into a great polo-playing family. His father is the great Gonzalo Pieres who was one of the first polo players to start to make a living out of playing polo.

'Polo is my life. Hopefully my whole future will evolve around polo! My father is a big horse breeder and my brothers and I are also starting to get involved in breeding. It's nice to be able to keep a family tradition going!

'Being a professional polo player means that you have to adjust and fit into a team quickly. You could be playing together in the same team during one tournament whereas in the next you might be playing against some players you were playing with before. Sometimes you will be playing with friends and sometimes you get to play with people you haven't played with before. Playing polo is the best way of making friends!'

Jack 'Rookie' Baillieu,
savouring a quiet moment in
Garangula, November 2003.
Rookie played for
Ellerston and the team lost
the final to the home team:
Urs and Guy Schwarzenbach,
Simon Keyte and JP Clarkin.
'I'm waiting for the
chukka to start, enjoying the
magnificent scenary. I love
playing in Australia. It's
home!'

Simon Keyte,
Garangula 2003.

New Zealand player Simon Keyte has been working at Urs Schwarzenbach's polo organization, Garangula, in Australia since the age of sixteen. 'I first got a job grooming for Garangula through my uncle who was playing for the team at the time. I soon started playing for Garangula and I still do now. I love it there!'

During the English high-goal season, however, Simon comes over to England. He is based at Urs' farm in Shiplake. He does help out with the horses there and supports Black Bears whenever he can. Yet Simon is also free to play for other patrons like the Vesteys or Tony Pidgley.

In this photo Simon is sandwiched between Glen Gilmore and Damien Johnston, two players that used to work for Garangula. 'Glen and I have to play against each other very often. Glen just hates it! When we played for Garangula, we won seventeen matches straight, never losing a game from September through to March! Damien and I were also team-mates for five years. Both are now playing for Bernard Roux's team Hyde Hill and I've got one of them either side of me!'

Simon is on a little New Zealand-bred horse called Dubbo. 'Dubbo was bought for 900 dollars in a little town called Dubbo! She's one of the best horses we have had at Garangula. Dubbo hasn't travelled to England because she has had a slight injury to one of her front legs. She is really special and you actually would expect to be paying 50,000 dollars for a horse of her quality!'

Damien Johnston, Hyde Hill, and Simon Keyte, Garangula, in the 2003 semi-final at Garangula. Damian, riding Jay, is on the ball while Simon is keeping a close watch, ready to challenge him.

Damien, now playing for Hyde Hill, used to work at Garangula during the 1990s.

'For three years I worked only part time during the winter months at Garangula because I was also playing at the Berwick Club in Melbourne at the time. Then I stayed there full time for a further four years, training the young horses as well as playing for the team. Together with Urs we won the Dudley Cup in Sydney which is one of the major Australian tournaments. I also won the Garangula tournament with Urs a couple of times in the mid-nineties. I loved it in Garangula. And still do! The facilities are great. Compared to Ellerston, it's got more of a homely feeling; I feel comfortable there. The springtime, when they have their tournament there, is the most beautiful time of the year.'

Simon Keyte comments on this photo. 'The little horse I am on is called Hockey Sticks. She was bought in New Zealand. Javier Astrada played her in the 2002 Gold Cup, the year Black Bears won. After that she got sent home because she had a funny foot. Damien and I have been friends for years and when we play against each other we just play as hard and as safely as we can. We just get on with it!

'When fighting for the ball, all I think of is that I have to win this play because you have to also think about the consequences should you not win it. Usually they are not very good; the other team could be scoring! I try to overpower my opponent whether he is my best mate or not!'

Canadian Fred Mannix charging down the field during the
2004 Queen's Cup final. This image was shot with a very slow
shutter speed to give an even greater sense of the velocity at
which players and ponies travel.

During the 2003 English polo season, Fred Mannix and Adrian Kirby put together the Millarville-Atlantic team. Silvestre Donavon and Julio Zavaleta joined them.

Fred started playing polo at the age of twelve. Up until Labegorce asked him to join them for the 2004 Queen's Cup, Fred had only ever played for his own team.

'The first season I got my expenses paid was 2004.'

At present Fred is studying business management in Florida.

'I have to take care of my studies first before I decide whether I want to turn professional. I found the school that was closest to polo though! This made my parents happy and I am happy too!

'In 2003 we played the Prince of Wales Cup, the Queen's Cup and the Warwickshire Cup. To tell you the truth it was a disaster! The ponies were not organized and the barn was disorganized too. We didn't agree with one another as players. So it didn't come as much of a surprise that we only won three games out of fourteen! To be fair it was a last minute thing and this is probably why it didn't really work.'

In this shot Fred is on Beauty, a mare he bought in England that year.

'I took her back to the US and played her in the sixth chukka during the US Open. She is amazing! I always play her in the sixth. She is one of my best.'

(Left and below) Agustin Nero, playing for Italy at the 2003 European Championships, Dallas Burston. Agustin's father is Italian, which allowed him to represent Italy.

'I found getting used to the fields and the different grass you have in England quite difficult. Also, I was told that 2003 had been quite a dry year; I found the ground very hard.

'Playing for Italy was special because I was representing a country but on the other hand I also looked at it as just a tournament.

'We lost to England in the final. They killed us! We started off very poorly and England just pulled away with a four-goal difference and we just never managed to catch up with them.'

In the second photo, Agustin is ahead of Dutch player Pablo van der Brink.

'The Holland match was different. We won that!'

(Opposite) Will Lucas and Fred Mannix on Cartier Day 2002. The Rest of the Commonwealth team took the Coronation Cup from England.

Will, cousin of Mark and Luke Tomlinson, played in his first Pony Club polo tournament at the age of twelve. After having worked for four years in commercial property, Will decided to become a polo professional at twenty-two.

'Initially I wanted to try my hand at full-time polo for two years with the view to going back to property but I never did go back. I then played seven seasons in Argentina and now I have a place in New Zealand. There I source horses, produce them and bring them over to England. This is one of my New Zealand thoroughbred mares. She wears a sheepskin over the top of her bridle, a trademark everybody seems to know her by. She is one of my best ponies. She is incredibly fast and handles very well too. I always love playing her because she is so low to the ground which makes it very easy to hit the ball. She is a very big-hearted mare. I feel privileged to have her in my yard.'

'Awesome' is the way Fred remembers the day he won the Coronation Cup. 'It was really great, especially as I had never been at Guards to play before. I experienced everything England had to offer on that particular day.'

Ryan Conroy, Nothern Ireland, leading his pony off the field after his morning match against the North Cotswold.

Ryan grew up around ponies; his mother Donna owns and runs a riding school and pony-trekking centre in Fivemiletown, Co. Tyrone. Donna admits not knowing much about polo and it was only thanks to Ryan getting invited to an introductory polo day that he got a chance to have a go.

'Ryan loved it from the word go. He is very keen and is hoping to make it to senior level. He is very outgoing and loves meeting people.'

In 2003 Ryan captained his team at the National Polo Championships at Cowdray. Northern Ireland won the Handley Cross section two.

Charlie Aprahamian went to Cowdray for the 2003 National Pony Polo Championship to support his brother Bill who was competing for the Grafton in the Handley Cross section. Charlie, ten in 2003, competed in the Jorrocks section. That final took place two days prior to the Handley Cross section, in Hurtwood, Surrey. At Cowdray, Charlie and friends were practising their stick and ball game on bicycles.

According to Charlie's mother, Bronwen: 'They do it all summer long. The boys live, breath, eat and sleep polo! One might even go as far as to say that they are a touch obsessed with polo! They play together and conduct little games. I'm sure it's really good for their hand/eye coordination. Mind you, Charlie's bicycle is probably more obedient than his pony but then again, the chances of him falling over with his bicycle are greater too!'

Charlie does not come from a polo-playing familiy. His father John did, however, compete for the Irish junior three-day-event team in Rome, 1974. The whole family is keen on hunting.

(Below) Nicholas De Lisle, Cottesmore Blue, on Bubbles during the 2003 National Pony Club finals, Cowdray.

Cottesmore Blue played Old Berkshire for the Handley Cross section, which is played over two chukkas. The first chukka always gets played in the morning on a smaller field and the second one in the afternoon on lawn one. In 2003 Old Berkshire got the better of Cottesmore and won the match 2–1. Goals scored in the morning get carried forward to the afternoon chukka. Old Berkshire won the morning chukka by 1–nil and the afternoon chukka ended 1–1.

Polo manager Jane Winterton believes that games are won in the morning. 'In the afternoon you have the parade of all the Pony Club teams. Ponies get wound up and there is a real sense of excitement. Players and ponies can either grow to it or go to pieces!'

In 2004 Cottesmore Blue reached the final again. This time they played Grafton and they made sure they learned from the previous year. They won the morning chukka 4–nil and pulled it off. The final score was 4–1.

Nicholas, who was twelve in 2003, comes from a very horsy family. His father, Edwin De Lisle is chairman of the Rutland Polo Club and his mother, Caroline, used to event. 'Nicholas loves polo but he is quite laid back about it. As for Bubbles, he is an all-rounder, good at all the required Pony Club activities but, like Nicholas, also enjoys polo the most!'

Edward Winterton, Cottesmore Blue, on his twenty-year-old pony Merlin during the final of the Handley Cross section at the National Pony Club finals, Cowdray 2003.

Edward decided he wanted to play polo at the age of five, when he saw a polo match and thought it so 'different from all the other activities one can do on a horse'. He thinks that polo is so unusual, very fast and really enjoyable. In 2003, aged thirteen, Edward played off a minus-one handicap, which is the upper limit for any child to be allowed in the Handley Cross section. The age limit for children is fourteen and the ponies should not measure more than 14.2 hh.

Playing at four, Edward was the sweeper. 'I like this position especially as I don't mind having the responsibilty of being the one who has the job of closing the door.'

Being a farmer's son Edward also enjoys hunting. His mother Jane, team manager of the Cottesmore Blue polo team, used to event. And Merlin, like any Handley Cross pony, enjoys all Pony Club activities. He hunts, show jumps, does Pony Club rallies and gets to play polo!

Dual of the patrons. Gillian
Johnston and Tony Pidgley
during the 2003 subsidiary
Queen's Cup semi-final. Gillian
is on a mare called Margot
that Miguel Novillo-Astrada
now plays.

Gillian and Miguel also
play together in the USA
where her team now
competes under the name of
her farm in Tennessee,
Bendabout.

'We run our polo breeding
operation there and have just
started our first year of
embryo transplant breeding.
Usually we perform pasture
breeding. We have thirty
mares and get between
twenty and twenty-five foals
a year.'

Gillian's biggest win came
in 2001 when she won the US
Open with her team, then
called Coca Cola.

HIGH-GOAL
PATRONS

For a sport to benefit from a backer is nothing too unusual. Having a benefactor who puts together a team of polo players as well as playing an active part within the team himself is, however, a slightly different matter and a situation unique to polo.

In the polo world this benefactor is called a 'patron'. He is the head of a polo team (sometimes also referred to as a polo organization) and therefore in charge of providing all that which is needed for a team to run successfully. To be more correct, perhaps, and to give a more realistic and accurate picture, the patron provides all the money that is needed to get the show off the ground!

A patron employs a polo manager who is put in charge of running the polo side of the patron's estate. He looks after the stables, the horses and the staff, usually consisting of a polo secretary, various groundsmen, lorry drivers and almost countless grooms. Depending on the set-up, the manager can also act as the link between the patron and his players.

The responsibilities of a polo manager are innumerable. Not only does he have to see to the well being of the polo ponies and prove his skills by communicating between vet, farrier and horses, he also has to be a good judge of people. The polo manager has to make sure that things are running smoothly for the professional polo players, which can get a bit tricky at times as some professionals have been known to be a touch demanding.

In addition, the polo manager has to organize the transportation of the horses, not only making sure that horses get to the polo grounds on time, but also making sure that horses travel safely from one country or continent to another. In the case of the high-goal team Labegorce, it means arranging for fifty-odd horses to make the journey from France to England a month prior to the opening of the English polo season and sending them back to France at the end of the season.

During the tournament, getting the team's 'corner' up and running with the tent and everything else that is needed also falls on the shoulders of the manager and his team of helpers. Everything has to be in place before the players and the patron arrive.

Everybody on the team of employees will have their work cut out; their duties will be organized and executed to perfection. The accomplishment of these tasks becomes even more amazing if you consider that most of a team's duties revolve around about forty, four-legged creatures during one polo match!

A polo set-up is often referred to as an organization simply because there is such a terrific amount of organizing to do! Being on the polo circuit and speaking to polo managers has certainly opened my eyes to the demands that go hand in hand with the job. It has also made it clear that the best-organized teams will, at the end of the day, be the ones that reap the top prizes.

High-goal polo is both an exciting yet also an expensive sport to be involved in. Imagine running a team of four polo players in a match that is played over six chukkas of seven minutes each. What this effectively means is that, as horses and players are going flat out trying to score goals, providing the necessary horsepower to enable the team to be competitive is of the utmost importance.

Patrons will always try to hire a key player who will act more or less as the pillar of the team. This player will on some occasions also take the role of team captain. Sometimes, as in the case of Black Bears' Urs Schwarzenbach, the role of the captain has also been taken by the patron. Generally speaking, the key player will look out for suitable team-mates and will put his ideas forward to the patron because the final decision will always be the patron's.

Finding suitable horses for the team also very often falls under the duties of the principal player. Being on the lookout for horses is such a big and continuous assignment that he will share this project with the polo manager and other people connected to a particular team.

Some patrons have taken to the idea of setting up their own breeding programme in order to provide themselves with a continuous flow of horses. Kerry Packer, Australian long-time patron of the eminent Ellerston team, has set the standard in realizing a successful breeding plan on his farm.

Most Argentine polo players are also very keen horse breeders. They do it not only because of their passion for horses and as something to do once they stop playing actively, but also many of them have a burning ambition to mount an entire team with homebred stock. Professional players have been known to sell their homebred horses to their patrons too.

A patron is, essentially, the person who picks up the tab for all the expenses and because of that he effectively becomes the employer, but the relationship between the patron and his players is built on the basis of friendship. This is not surprising as the team spends a lot of time together, planning, discussing and, not least, playing a fast and dangerous game that relies heavily on trust and mutual understanding. What is perhaps more surprising is that patrons who move in completely different circles most of the year, seem to truly enjoy the blend of diverse backgrounds and cultures they mix with while playing polo.

Furthermore, I have noticed that patrons are greatly respected by their employees. Some would even argue that polo would not be where it is now without everything the patrons put into the sport. Australian patron Kerry Packer has put a lot of research into improving the quality of polo fields, and his efforts have been recognized worldwide, particularly by those players who have been fortunate enough to play on his fields during the

Ellerston tournaments. Some other patrons have followed suit. Urs Schwarzenbach, to name only one, has also built outstanding facilities both at Garangula, his farm in Australia, and at his set-up in Shiplake, Oxfordshire.

As this book focuses on the top end of the sport, I have tried to get a better feeling and a deeper understanding for what kind of people high-goal polo-playing patrons are. In order to find out what makes these people tick and why they are in the game of polo, I spoke to two highly successful patrons. One is Hubert Perrodo, French patron of Labegorce and a winner of countless trophies. The other is Ali Albwardi, successful patron of Dubai and also a winner of numerous events.

Speaking to both men, I found out that what they undoubtedly have in common is a love for horses, an addiction to speed and an almost unquenchable thirst for winning!

Both are extremely accomplished businessmen, and both are aware of their ambitions and are driven by a strong desire to leave their mark in life. When transferred to polo, their energies are directed towards building the best possible polo organization.

Hubert Perrodo is a man motivated not only by his enjoyment for changing things but, more to the point, he is also always trying to improve everything he puts his mind to.

Entrepreneur, Ali Albwardi, is also keen to progress in all projects he turns his hand to and, by being the dynamic person he is, success is never far away.

As the following pages reveal, both men are fascinating, and I hope that you will find their philosophy of life as inspiring as I do.

Labegorce and its Patron Hubert Perrodo

'Playing practice chukkas in the morning sets me up for the day!' Hubert Perrodo, a charming man full of joie de vivre, is the French patron of the highly successful high-goal team, Labegorce. Like so many people, Hubert needs a feeling of balance, fullness and tranquility in his life. The rush of adrenaline he derives from riding at speed and skilfully controlling a horse while working around seven other polo ponies, gives Hubert just that. And what better setting in which to satisfy his needs than the beautifully idyllic, peaceful and harmonious surroundings of Anningsley Park, a property Hubert bought some eight years ago. Situated in Surrey approximately twenty minutes from Heathrow and forty minutes from his London office, it is also central to both the Guards and Cowdray Polo Clubs, homes to the two major polo tournaments Labegorce has been competing in for the past sixteen years.

The team's consistent efforts and Hubert's passion for the game have thankfully, and in a way inevitably, lead to numerous titles. However, it hasn't

Labegorce patron,
Hubert Perrodo.

Hubert Perrodo has been involved in polo for some sixteen years and he loves it. He describes it as: 'A team sport which greatly depends on the horses you play; it is a sport with endless scope for improvement.'

been plain sailing right from the start and Hubert recalls with humour how it all began.

Introduced to polo by a sailing friend, Hubert remembers his first attempt: 'I could not hold a horse let alone make it go where I wanted it to go!' And, when he eventually got back to the stables the polo instructor said that he thought that Hubert was a bit too old to take up the sport, but he did not read Hubert's character correctly. 'Annoyed by the instructor's comments, I started to play.' Initially Hubert just wanted to play with friends. 'However, polo is a sport that soon becomes a passion.' For this reason, as well as his love of competing, Hubert took

his team into high-goal polo almost immediately. 'It was awful actually because I couldn't ride properly and I used to fall off two, three times in a match!' But, bitten by the sport and keen 'to fight for something', he persevered. Hubert found the game itself not too difficult to understand. 'It is fast, I will say that, but polo has similarities with other team sports.' He soon found out that success is 85-90 per cent down to the quality of a team's horses, and concluded that with good horses 'you have a tremendous head start'.

Realizing that he needed 'someone who was truly a pillar for the team' and determined to make his mark, Hubert initially got Horacio Heguy, a player who had won the Argentine Open countless times, to join his team. 'Horacio is an excellent player and I learned a lot about the game from him.'

Labegorce's first big wins soon began trickling in: the Queen's Cup in 1995 with team members Milo Fernandez-Araujo and Pepe Heguy (who stood-in for Horacio Heguy who had sadly lost one of his eyes in an accident); the Deauville Gold Cup, when it was still a twenty-two goal tournament; and in 1997 the team's name was engraved on the Cowdray Gold Cup too.

When asked what the winning formula for Hubert Perrodo and Labegorce is, he is quick to remark that his team is not the only one and that others have been just as successful. He points to Ellerston White, Black Bears and Dubai, and adds that there are always a few teams at the same level battling it out. Also, he admits to not really knowing why

Labegorce is successful but said this. 'Fundamentally it must be because the team is very well organized, has good horses, good players and countless hard-working people behind the scenes all contributing and therefore pulling in the same direction. Of course, there is still the game to play too and you can say that a team is lucky or unlucky but when you have reached all the semi-finals or finals for the past seven years, you know that you are doing something right! When you play polo at this level you have to set some priorities. The first one being that no one gets hurt. Secondly, no horses should get hurt. Thirdly, you want to play well. Wanting to win comes fourth. And, usually, when the first three apply the fourth one should be there too!'

One significant member of the winning team is Frenchman Ludovic Cressant, Hubert's polo manager since 1992, who is of this opinion: 'Polo is a very complex sport that revolves around the horses, and, above all, what makes the real difference between winning and losing a match, if you have two teams of the same handicap and player ability, is the horsepower.'

Ludovic's job is not easy to describe and certainly does not equate to a nine to five job. He supervises the organization of the vet, the farrier and the travelling arrangements for the horses, ensuring, for example, that fifty polo ponies in France arrive at Anningsley Park a month before the beginning of the English high-goal polo season and get back to France soon after the final of the Cowdray Gold Cup.

In France, Hubert has another set-up near Bordeaux in the Medoc region where the horses stay and rest for the remainder of the year. This property is where Hubert's other interest, his vineyard, has also been established, and it too is called Labegorce. When Hubert started in polo most patrons were using their business names for their teams, and so he decided to use the name of his vineyard.

On a bigger scale one could actually transfer Hubert's polo ideology to life in general. He is, after all, a self-made man who started his business at the age of twenty-nine, and now has some 4000 people in twelve countries working for him.

Hubert, however, does not consider this to be remarkable; he simply calls it 'good fun'. Well, that leads me to believe that maybe there are no real secrets to victory!

This is Hubert's firmly held belief: 'If you want to succeed in life you have to first of all bring some talent along, whatever that talent may be for: business or polo. Then, it is about working, working hard and a need for determination. All this put together soon turns into passion. You find yourself passionate about what it is you want to achieve and suddenly you don't consider it as work anymore. You enjoy it.'

The patron of Black Bears, Urs Schwarzenbach, giving Hubert Perrodo last minute encouragement before Labegorce played Dubai in the 2003 final of the Queen's Cup.

'Urs probably told me that I should win the match because this is what we always say to each other when one of us is in a final! I like Urs a lot; he is the patron I spend the most time with. I have fun with him. And his wife Francesca is such a lovely lady too!'

He points out: 'When you build a team and you have done it properly, it all starts to work'. Also, he adds, 'Never forget to keep people (and horses!) happy and they will keep on working for you, and

Hubert is having a chat with Lolo Castagnola and Adolfo Cambiaso after having lost the 2003 Queen's Cup by the narrowest of margins to Dubai.

'I wasn't too graceful in defeat this particular time. I was actually very upset because we should have won. It came down to an umpire's bad decision and it's funny because one week later a member of the umpiring committee called me to apologize. After that I was happier and we moved on. Cambiaso told me that I shouldn't think that we deserved to lose that day. This was a nice gesture. Still, I was very upset at the time because I hate injustice, no matter the circumstance.'

more importantly they will give you their best.'

Hubert applied the same concept to his vineyard which, considering its size, has become much more than just a pastime. Labegorce now produces more than 250,000 bottles of wine a year. 'When I took it on in 1988, round about the same time as I got into polo, the place was in ruins. We built it up and now it is a recognized wine! And, that's a lot of fun!'

In the same way as polo players refer to their sport as a way of life, so too will Hubert insist that the wine business creates a way of life because 'you simply cannot go faster than the seasons'.

Meeting Hubert and judging by the way he goes through life it is easy to believe that he is very happy when he gets into the office. He explains that he enjoys it when things fall into place because of

how he and his team have approached and solved issues. However, he is also quick to admit that if he hasn't had his fair share of physical exercise or a certain number of chukkas under his belt, he can become difficult and demanding!

The man in charge of seeing that Hubert enjoys polo as much as possible is none other than Mexican polo magician and exemplary polo professional Carlos Gracida.

Carlos and Hubert had known each other for a good while before the time was right for the two men to join forces. Carlos recalls the first time he played against Hubert. 'It was a league match for the Gold Cup which incidentally was also Adolfo Cambiaso's first ever match in England and, although we started off really poorly we did manage to beat Hubert. I immediately liked Hubert, I thought he was a very nice man.'

Carlos was amazed that although Hubert used to lose nine games out of ten he was still nice to his professionals and remembers saying to himself, 'Just imagine how happy Hubert will be if he starts winning!' One year before the Gold Cup final Hubert told Carlos that he liked his spurs, and so Carlos said that he would give them to him after the match. Carlos won the Gold Cup and, as promised, gave Hubert his spurs!

Now that they are actually working towards achieving the same goals their relationship has deepened even more. Hubert trusts Carlos with finding and organizing the horses. Carlos will suggest possible team members but reveals: 'We make

the decisions together so we cannot blame one another!'

Carlos believes that one of the keys to their success lies in the horses they manage to get. Hubert is very supportive and Carlos feels that they have done well although there is still room for improvement, particularly as the aim is to be the best team of the best teams!

Finding the best horses is an ongoing process. The face of polo is changing and, although Carlos does play horses that belong to Hubert, the

tendency for the professionals to mount themselves is on the up. Playing for more than one patron heightens the challenge of finding quality horses. At one time Carlos was winning in England, Argentina and the USA all at the same time. That's an awful lot of horses!

It is no wonder, therefore, that Carlos admits to having a good eye for horses. He even goes as far as to say, 'I am a better judge of horses than I am a player.' I suppose being as well mounted as he has been over the past twenty years illustrates his point.

A dynamic photo of Hubert Perrodo during the 2003 Queen's Cup final. On seeing it Hubert commented: 'I should lose a bit of weight to make it easier for the horse! But I can also see that I have improved my position, or I might just be thinking that because it is a great photo?'

Carlos Gracida on the ball in a league match against Larchmont during the 2004 Queen's Cup tournament. This year, together with Labegorce, Carlos finally managed to pull off the Queen's Cup victory he was so longing for.

'I really thought I was never going to win it. I tried not to put myself under pressure and told myself, "Listen if you don't win it's not the end of the world. You have won every other major tournament so just relax!" When we won, it was such a big relief! I never wanted to retire and have people say that I had won every major tournament but the Queen's Cup.'

When it came to the actual prize-giving ceremony, a very compassionate Hubert sent Carlos to accept the trophy from the Queen on behalf of Labegorce.

'No other patron had ever wanted me to receive the trophy on behalf of his team. It really touched me.'

The criteria Carlos looks out for are very simple. 'Class! Speed, stamina and intelligence come into it too.' He does, therefore, always tend to favour pure thoroughbred racehorses. Even if they have not raced or made it to the top in racing, Carlos

most difficult sport in the world, so try and make it easier!' And, Carlos insists, 'This also means making it easier for your team-mates!' Of course Labegorce will have team talks but Carlos will always be primarily in favour of team-mates being friends.

Patron Hubert Perrodo on the attack against Geebung in Labergorce's quarter-final match for the 2004 Queen's Cup.

maintains that they still have good bloodlines. 'In fact, I prefer it they haven't raced. A horse is like a child. You don't want to spoil or abuse it. Further, a horse has to be naturally balanced and keep his balance in every situation. Whether it is when stopping, turning, going sideways or flat out. You cannot fight nature. Either the horse has the right components or not.'

A part of Carlos's adopted polo philosophy stems from his father who used to tell him, 'Polo is the

They have dinners, barbecues and watch polo videos together, all with the aim of putting players at ease and to create a good atmosphere within the team.

In the polo world Carlos is recognized as the best horseman around, which is not surprising if his ancestry is considered. His grandfather used to play polo for the Mexican army and was in charge of breaking-in up to 300 horses a year. 'He was a true master and I wish I knew half as much as he did. Sadly, I think that in a way a lot of my grandfather's

Luke Tomlinson, Carlos Gracida, Fred Mannix and patron Hubert Perrodo are celebrating their 2004 Queen's Cup victory. Hubert had won the Queen's Cup before, nonetheless this win was very special!

'We were very happy to win! I think we played very solid polo as a team. The win was very important for Carlos. He had won all the major tournaments except the Queen's Cup. He was starting to believe that there was a spell on it. It took us four finals and this time Carlos managed. I felt very happy, not only for the team but especially for Carlos!

'I think Azzurra played very well too. We had very good horses and the difference showed in the last two chukkas when our horses were magnificent. When you know that the horses are going well you have less pressure. Yet we had moments when I thought "no, not again", like when I had an under-the-neck shot towards goal and it hit the post. In the last chukka, Luke broke away and he was halfway down the field; we were leading by one goal and I thought, "if he gets that one in we are OK". Then his mallet broke and, again, I thought, "oh no, what next?" But, we managed to hold onto our lead and we won. It was just an excellent feeling!'

knowledge got lost through the generations.'

Carlos's brother, Memo Gracida, proved to be another huge influence and, thanks to his brother's brilliance and immense success, Carlos decided to embark on a polo career instead of becoming an architect.

'My brother inspired me and opened the doors. He went to the US with the Mexican polo team and won the Camacho Cup which Mexico had never won before. Memo became my idol. I love playing with Memo. His record speaks for itself. He is one of the all-time greats and to top it I can call him my brother. What more can you ask for than to be playing with him.'

I could think of one thing immediately, and that was winning the Queen's Cup which in Carlos's

own illustrious career had eluded him until June 2004 when, together with Fred Mannix, Luke Tomlinson and patron Hubert Perrodo, he finally managed to put his hands on this prestigious trophy.

Even so, Carlos talks about the horses being more important to him than the game, or winning for that matter. 'As a player you are just a passenger. Even if you are the best player, people will forget you sooner or later so if you base your happiness or values on your achievements you are wasting your time. The horse, on the other hand, is the most noble animal there is.'

Another vital lesson both his father and grandfather taught him, and one that Carlos is keen to pass on, was that, without using one's legs one cannot create a communication with the horse. 'Of course you do have to use the reins a bit too but more than fifty per cent of your communication has to come from your legs!'

Labegorce might not yet be the best of the best but, when taking into account all the expertise and the determination at hand, not to mention the fun and excitement polo creates, it becomes quite clear why Labegorce *is* the team it is!

Dubai and its Patron Ali Saeed Albwardy

'Polo is worse than a drug! If you have a drug problem you can seek help from a doctor and he could heal you. With polo there are only two reasons you quit: one, you go bankrupt and run out of money, and the other is, you die. There is no third reason!'

As there is no chance that highly successful businessman and patron of the mighty Dubai polo team, Ali Saeed Albwardy, will ever run out of money, his team will thankfully grace the lawns of Guards and Cowdray for many years to come. Ali is more than passionate about his favourite sport. 'I think I am the only person who plays polo 365 days a year.' After playing the high-goal season in England, Ali plays in Dubai at his amazing facilities, and there the season lasts nine months! I am sure you get the picture by now: Ali 'just can't get enough of it!'

In 2004, London-based Ham Polo Club asked Ali to be their president, a position he sees as a great

opportunity to introduce as many people to polo as possible. 'I have already introduced more than fifty people and they all say that it is the best thing that has ever happened to them. Polo is just beautiful and you don't have to be a champion to enjoy it.'

Ali started to play polo just with friends some twenty years ago before deciding ten years later to come and compete in England. At first, Dubai began to play the low- and medium-goal tournaments and Ali remembers that after they had won twenty-five cups in one season the time was right for him to move his team up to high goal. He believes that you have to achieve something before you can move up. He soon realized that playing the English high goal is very hard! Ali stresses, 'It is horses, horses, horses and you can't just go out and buy them. It takes time to build a team and a good string of polo ponies.' You also need a top player and, in Adolfo Cambiaso, Ali has just that. 'Adolfo is the best player in the world. He is like Schumacher, which means you have to give him a Ferrari, or rather a few Ferraris!'

Adolfo appreciates Ali's input enormously and confirms that should he ever need a horse he doesn't even have to ask. 'Ali will give it to me. Also, if Ali needs a horse I will give it to him. It is not one-sided and never a problem.'

In terms of horsepower, Ali suggests that Dubai have the best horses, which has taken time to achieve. As a team they are always on the look-out for good horses and find them in New Zealand, the USA and Argentina. 'Giving my players the best

Ali Saaed Albwardi, patron of Dubai.

possible horses means that they can play their handicap.'

Also, let us not forget that partnering Cambiaso, and a major contributing factor to Dubai's success, is his brother-in-law Lolo Castagnola, also a ten-goal player.

Ali, however, is quick to point out that Dubai 'is not just a team it is an organization'. In polo circles people will always refer to their team as an organization and claim that the better the organization the higher the chances of being successful. What effectively is meant by 'organization' in this context, is the whole infrastructure, the set-up and the countless people working behind the scenes. According to Ali, the formula for success is simple. 'It comes down to the infrastructure, the horses, the players, the grooms and how you combine all of those ingredients.'

The question remains, however, how do you get hold of the right components? Adolfo Cambiaso and Ali have been good friends for a long time. Ali recalls that when Adolfo was still playing for Kerry Packer, they had always agreed that eventually they wanted to play together. So, Ali waited until Adolfo was available and the day Cambiaso became free he joined Ali. Lolo Castagnola had joined Dubai two years earlier and, although they don't necessarily come as a package, it is hard to think of Lolo and Adolfo apart, let alone to imagine Dubai without the pair.

Ali is happy to refer to his players as his friends and proud to announce that Cambiaso is not bound to Dubai by contract. Although Adolfo constantly

Dubai with the 2001 Veuve Cliquot Gold Cup trophy. Ryan Pemble, played alongside Adolfo Cambiaso and Lolo Castagnola for patron Ali Saaed Albwardi.

'Winning is great because it is the achievement of a goal you have set yourself and have worked towards. Nothing can be better than that.'

Replacing his father Ali Albwardi as the number one player, Tariq Albwardi was brought into the Dubai team at the beginning of the 2004 Veuve Cliquot Gold Cup tournament. The then sixteen-year-old proved his talent and love for the game of polo. Here Tariq wins the battle for the ball against his counterpart, Stefano Marsaglia, patron of Azzurra during the final, which Azzurra won.

gets offers to play elsewhere he has told Ali that he does not want to play anywhere else during the English season. Ali even goes as far as saying that the day Cambiaso leaves Dubai might be the day Ali will stop playing competitively.

Ali doesn't like the high profile that inevitably gets associated with polo. 'I am not interested in the luxury. I love the game and I love horses.'

During the three months that Ali is in England the game of polo does, however, only mean one thing: winning! The excitement comes with the prospect of winning the Queen's Cup and the Gold Cup. He has of course achieved both these aims and

wants to see the Dubai name engraved on both magnificent trophies again and again.

As well as being patron, Ali is also the captain of his team. Cambiaso is in charge of team tactics and of trying out players to fit in as fourth man. Every year from the beginning of May, four to five players are put through their paces and looked at as potential team-mates for the following season. Once a choice has been made, those who can will go over to Argentina to spend some time with Adolfo during the winter months. Ali explains: 'You don't buy players to make a profit as in football; in polo, you have to enjoy the members of your team.'

Ali Saaed Albwardi, patron
of Dubai, playing on his
home ground during a
league match for the 2003
Queen's Cup. In the early
stages of the Queen's Cup,
Guards Polo Club assigns
some games to teams that
have wonderful facilities
and are willing to host
matches.

Robert Thame, polo manager for Dubai, helped out during the 2004 subsidiary semi-final of the Queen's Cup.

New Zealander John Paul 'JP' Clarkin, playing for Cadenza, managed to keep his line. Cadenza proved to be a step ahead on the day.

Apart from the enjoyment, there is no doubt that what drives Ali most is winning. 'It is like in business, although you must not forget the moral side of things, you count your success on how much you make. Otherwise you never grow! The same goes for polo. The only way of knowing that you are successful is winning. It is proof of being on the right track.'

For Ali, England offers the best polo in the world. The two major tournaments he enters are steeped in history and become so very difficult to win because 'the best patrons in the world want to do the same'.

Nevertheless Ali claims that they are very relaxed as a team. His players have won everything there is to win, and so he knows they can do it. 'If we lose a game I am not going to fire them. Primarily they are my friends and as a patron you have to give your players confidence.' Some patrons change professionals when they lose but Ali doesn't think that this move is 'necessarily going to work miracles'. He says, 'Most of all, you have to give your professionals horses!' For Ali, it is like any other business; it takes time. It took him five years to get to where he is in polo.

Ali's advice to any newcomer who wants to compete at high-goal level, is not to rush into things and to give it time and, more importantly, 'Unless you have the money to back up your operation, don't come into polo.' When people tell Ali about cheap deals he simply replies, 'Why waste your time?'

Ali explains that there are also patrons who pump a lot into their polo yet they too lose because the spirit of the team is not there. Adolfo reinforces the importance of a good team spirit and puts Dubai's success down to a team spirit which he describes as being 'second to none'.

In order to succeed, Ali suggests that people do what he himself did. 'You analyse how patrons before you have done it. For me Kerry Packer is a great example. He has done it the right way; it took him seven years to win the Gold Cup. Urs Schwarzenbach of Black Bears has done it the right way too and has been rewarded with top trophies.'

Having a great polo manager, such as Robert Thame, also helps in the running of a good-spirited and well-organized operation. Robert has been with Ali right from the beginning of Ali's polo days in England. They met at Ham Polo Club and Robert, a four-goal freelance player at the time, started to play low- and medium-goal polo with Ali. In 1994, two years into playing tournaments, Ali bought some land in Holyport with the view of playing high goal

in 1997. Robert recalls that building the stables and creating the fields, as well as fighting to get various planning permissions, took the best part of two years. The 1995 season had gone extremely well for them. Dubai had won every tournament they had entered, sixty-five matches, and so they decided to move into high goal a year earlier than originally planned. For their first season, Ali picked Marcos Heguy, 'The best available player at the time.' Together with Lolo Castagnola they beat a few teams and made it to the subsidiary final of the Queen's Cup, but were beaten by Black Bears.

Robert remembers that they were really short of horses. 'The only good horses we had were Marcos's four which he had brought over and which we consequently ended up buying from him. But you cannot expect to compete with established teams early on even if you have a professional who is mounted on his own horses. Ali, Urs and Kerry are the patrons who make the difference because they buy the horses. Adolfo needs super horses and in general a professional cannot afford to mount himself as well as a patron can afford to mount him.'

Robert's job is to have everything up and running for when Adolfo and Lolo arrive in the second week in May. The horses will have already been in work for ten weeks and are 'ready to rock and roll'. 'Should they not be ready it equates to them losing the first tournament.' It is another part of Robert's job to organize practice matches during the early stages of a tournament because there can often be too many non-match days between

Sergio Casella, head groom for Dubai, winning his trophy after Dubai won the Queen's Cup in 2003. Sergio joined Dubai when they started competing at high-goal level and has been Dubai's head groom during the English high-goal season ever since. He spends the rest of the year in Argentina where he breeds and owns horses in partnership with Lolo Castagnola.

tournament matches. Robert also describes himself as being the link between the horses, the vet, and the farrier, and between the players and Ali should there be a complication. 'It is often easier for me to ask Ali for more money for the players or, the other way round, to tell the players "no". It is also easier for me to be the negotiator when buying horses.'

In Robert's eyes the winning formula comes in the shape of Adolfo Cambiaso because 'Any team that has Adolfo in it benefits from a head start!' He admits that because tournaments are played according to a handicap system, everybody is trying to cheat that system. 'You try to get a seven-goal player who is really an eight, or a one who is worth two. Adolfo beats the handicap system every time. Although there are a number of ten-goal players, he is better than them. On paper he is still only a ten but really he's more like a twelve!' Furthermore, Robert remarks that Adolfo wants to win probably more than Ali, which is saying a lot!

Managing the team in England is more demanding than running Ali's polo operation in Dubai itself. There Ali enjoys playing for fun with his sons and friends but here it is all about winning. 'If for any reason our best horse is injured, it's like cutting off a finger. If Adolfo's best horse was missing it would mean two chukkas out of six gone.'

Keeping polo ponies in top form takes much more than meets the eye. Robert compares the training of a polo pony with that of a racehorse. 'Any racehorse trainer will tell you that training the

Derby winner is easier than keeping a polo pony at its peak for the duration of the Queen's Cup. In racing they get the horse ready for the trials in early May and then for the race itself in June. We, on the

Ali Saaed Albwardi with the 2003 Queen's Cup Trophy.
'For me England offers the best polo in the world. England is full of history too and believe me, winning here is not easy!'

other hand, have to win a race twice a week for three weeks.'

And win they do! Ali and his 'Dubai polo organization' have won them all. As for Adolfo Cambiaso, he has played a key role in it all which makes him 'a very happy man' and he concludes: 'Should I ever leave Dubai I can be very happy to have helped Ali win the Indian Empire Shield, the Warwickshire Cup, the Queen's Cup and the Gold Cup.'

**Veuve Cliquot Gold Cup
final 2003.**

GROOMS – BEHIND THE SCENES

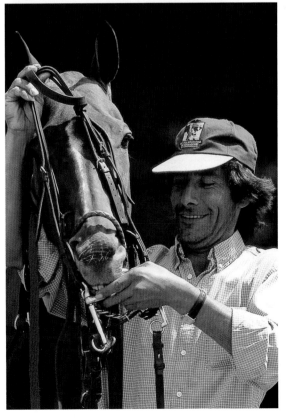

(Above) Ellerston 2004.

(Far left) Cirencester 2003.

(Left) Veuve Cliquot Gold Cup final 2003.

(Top left, right and below left)
Cirencester 2003.

(Below right)
Cowdray 2003.

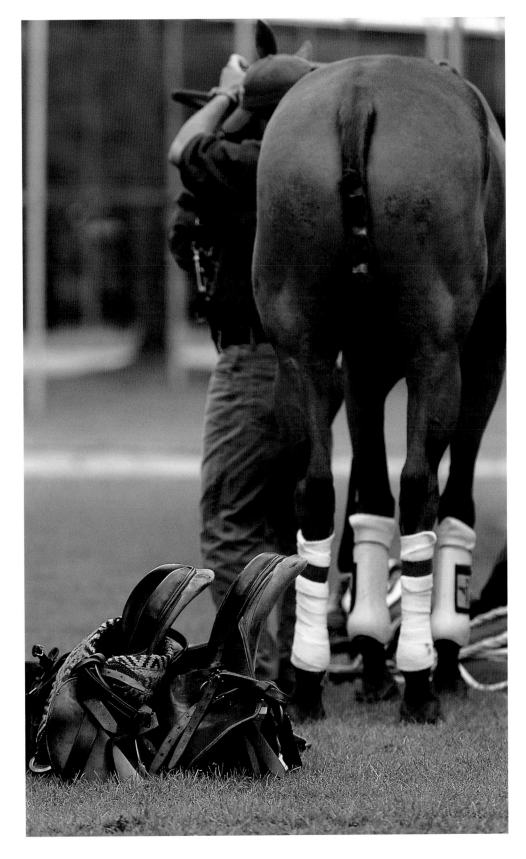

(Above) Deauville 2003.

(Left) Guards 2003.

Daniel Flores, Pepe Araya's groom, taking the ponies for an early morning swim in Deauville 2003.

An enjoyable moment for Pepe Araya's homebred mare, Nube, Deauville 2003.

(Above) Ellerston 2004.

(Above left) Early
morning, Ellerston 2004.

(Left) Garangula 2003.

(Right) Sotogrande 2004.

(Far right) Wastecorp
groom and pony before
the final, Ellerston 2004.

(Below) Sotogrande 2004.

(Left) Ellerston 2004.

(Below left) Sotogrande 2004.

(Below right) HB pony,
Deauville 2003.

Damien Johnston on Salarbre,
a mare he got for patron
Bernard Roux in Queensland.

In fact all Hyde Hill horses
belong to the patron.
Damien's job is to find the
team's horses. Often he buys
young horses that he then
trains.

'I really enjoy green
horses. I like playing green
horses' chukkas and seeing
the horses progress. I still
love winning tournaments too
but I get the biggest thrill
out of making three- to four-
year-old horses. When buying
horses, I look for a good
temperament above all, then
comes conformation and size.
By good temperament I
mean, nice, calm and cool! I
don't like them hot. Also, I
try not to buy chestnuts!
Generally, I prefer mares, they
are more consistant. However,
if you get a good gelding, he
can be as good as any mare.
Salarbre is a good mare to
play, she tries really hard.

'What I love most about
polo is the horses. We have
also started a breeding
programme over the past two
years. I enjoy that a lot and
am looking forward to
breaking-in our first foals. We
have nine brood mares and
we have also just embarked
on our first embryo
transplant.

'As for Ellerston, I have
been going there since it
started in 1988-89 You
almost take it for granted!
The fields are simply a
benchmark!'

POLO IN ACTION

Damien Johnston, Hyde Hill, on his way towards goal at Ellerston during the 2004 J.D. Macleod Cup subsidiary final against Garangula.

Damien has been with Bernard Roux, patron of Hyde Hill, since September 1999. He manages all of the Hyde Hill horses at his own farm in Queensland.

'Whenever, and wherever, the polo is on, I turn up lock, stock and barrel! Truck, horses and grooms are all in place at the venue. All ready for Bernard to turn up at the tournament.

'We were a bit unlucky in the J.D. Macleod tournament. We lost the semi-final to Ellerston in overtime, and went on to win the subsidiary against Garangula. Actually, Garangula led for most of the match but we got our momentum in the fifth and slowly picked back at them in the fifth and sixth chukkas. The mare I'm on is a New Zealand thoroughbred called Sylvie. She is one of our best horses. She is fabulous. She even makes me look good! She is push button, automatic. She does practically everything you ask of her!'

Santiago Chavanne has been a professional polo player since 1998. He is good friends with Adolfo Cambiaso and Lolo Castagnola.

'I have a farm next to theirs and I started playing polo with them. They have helped me along.'

The third season Santiago played in England was in 2004, and it was the first time he brought his own horses over. It was also the first time he played for French patron Edouard Carmignac and Talandracas in the Gold Cup.

In this, the second match Talandracas played in the Gold Cup tournament, Santiago is fighting for the ball with Henry Brett.

'We were unfortunate to lose to Cadenza in overtime. Here I am winning the ball from Henry though!'

Santiago Chavanne, playing for Talandracas, and about to score a goal against Beaufort in the final of the 2004 Ashton Silver Cup, a subsidiary of the Gold Cup. Satnam Dhillon is just a bit too far away to prevent Santiago from putting the ball through the posts.

'During the match my team-mate Guillermo Terrera had a bad fall and we had to substitute another player for him. It was a close match and again we lost in overtime. But we had a great season! I really enjoyed playing for Edouard. He is a great patron. In 2005 we are aiming to start our season playing the Queen's Cup and then play the Gold Cup.'

Eduardo Novillo-Astrada
trying to hit a bouncing ball
during the final of the 2003
Argentine Open in Palermo.

'I got a pass from Javier and
overtook Lolo travelling in the
direction of the goal. The ball
bounced so I had to hit it in
the air. I made good contact
but it went just wide of the
goal by half a metre. This was
in the third chukka and I'm
on my Chilean thoroughbred
mare called Solitud. I also
played her in England in 2002,
the year we won the Gold Cup
with Black Bears.'

(Above and right) Lolo Castagnola, La Dolfina, measuring up a backhand close to the boards. Eduardo Novillo-Astrada is anticipating Lolo's move yet he couldn't prevent Lolo from striking the ball in the direction of the goal.

The 2003 final of the Argentine Open was a tightly contested match between La Dolfina and La Aguada. The Argentine Open is played over eight chukkas. Players can be on the field up to two hours which, as Eduardo explains, 'can take its toll'. 'It gets very tough mentally. Also, in Palermo you get more tired because of the importance the Open represents to us. It's a great occasion, and together with the setting you feel an extra rush of adrenaline! It definitely adds another dimension to your game. It's just amazing and I always get goose bumps!'

Lolo feels that La Dolfina lost the final because: 'We had to lose it. A lot of things didn't go right before the final. The crowd upset the final by invading the field for almost an hour, delaying the match. This upset me. Losing Esperanza, one of my best horses, in the sixth chukka, added to my unhappiness; I felt like crying. It's very difficult to explain. And I didn't understand why things were going against us. We were winning by two in the sixth chukka and then we lost. The Astradas deserved to win though because they were the only team that played well together every match they played. They were so hungry to win and it all fell into place for them.'

(Right) Two Astrada brothers – Javier, Black Bears, and Nacho, Geebung – playing against each other during a league match for the 2004 Queen's Cup. The match was played at Shiplake, Black Bears home ground.

Nacho, having the slight advantage over Javier, managed to hit an under-the-neck shot which Javier could not intercept.

This was Nacho's first high-goal season in England. He is also the only Astrada who hasn't, thus far, played for Black Bears.

(Below) Javier Novillo-Astrada during the 2003 final in Palermo, home to the Argentine Open.

Owing to the heat, the games are usually scheduled to start late in the afternoon by which time the sun is quite low. The showground is surrounded by high buildings and after the second chukka the sun starts hiding behind a huge block of flats. In this photo the shadow is beginning to creep in.

'I was knocking the ball back into play from the left and then unleashed a passing shot. When you get a good hold of the ball it can travel far! I remember that once during a match in Palermo I hit a goal from the halfway line galloping flat out. I had aimed at the goal because there were only a few seconds remaining in the match. The ball crossed the goal line with a second to go! This gives any player a truly amazing feeling! This shot too certainly looks as if it went far!'

Javier Novillo-Astrada in dire straits during the 2003 Gold Cup quarter-final between Black Bears and Graffham.

'I had just hit an under-the-neck shot pretty close to the boards and was trying to turn Shimmer. However, we were probably too close to the boards really, and so she ended up jumping over the boards. Shimmer is a New Zealand thoroughbred mare and belongs to Black Bears. She is amazing. She won Best Playing Pony at the 2002 Gold Cup Final.'

Javier Novillo-Astrada, Black
Bears, and Adrian Kirby,
Atlantic, fighting for the ball
just in front of the goal
during the 2004 Indian
Empire Shield trophy final.

'I'm on Misty K, one of my
better mares. We had never
entered that tournament
before so it was great to win
it at our first attempt! To
reach the final we had to win
by ten goals and we won by
twelve which was fabulous!
Eduardo and I played
alternately in each match.
Winning the semis was down
to him, Urs, Sebastian Dawnay
and Nicolas Vieri. In this
picture I am just getting
hooked in front of the
goalmouth, I did manage to
get to the ball but then
another yellow shirt just
saved the ball from crossing
the line!'

Miguel Novillo-Astrada and Adolfo Cambiaso during the 2003 Argentine Open final.

'Playing against Adolfo can be very difficult. You have to concentrate hard and be very alert when marking him because he is very fast and he has very good mallet control. You don't want to be too clever when he is close to you. Here, he is marking me; you should not be on the ball for too long when he is around in case he gets the ball off you. With this in mind I shot towards the goal and I scored! I scored two goals under the neck riding that same horse. She is called Califa. I bought her as a five-year-old and made her. I remember practising that shot a lot the day before!'

Guillermo Terrera, Cadenza, and Miguel Novillo-Astrada, Graffham, during the 2003 subsidiary semi-final of the Queen's Cup.

'I remember that we lost! My job was to mark Miguel Novillo-Astrada and, I can assure you, it is almost impossible to mark him because he is such an intelligent player. I would say he is one of the most clever players I have played.'

Guillermo has been coming to England since 2002 when he played with Eduardo and Javier Novillo-Astrada for Black Bears.

'We reached the semis of the Queen's Cup that year and lost to the eventual winners, Emerging. For the Gold Cup, which Black Bears went on to win, Alejandro Novillo-Astrada played instead of me.'

Marcos Heguy and Ignacio 'Nacho' Novillo-Astrada during the 2003 Argentine Open semi-final. La Aguada beat Indios Chapaleufu I. Marcos is on his way to goal while Nacho is trying to save the situation.

'Marcos ended up scoring there. It was a bit unfortunate for me but, in fairness, Marcos was not the player I was supposed to mark and I tried to recover the situation but I couldn't prevent Marcos from scoring after all!'

Guillermo Terrera played for Talandracas in 2004; the team lost to Larchmont in the quarter-final of the Gold Cup.

Guillermo, only twenty years old in 2004, won the Copa Potrillos, the most important Argentine tournament for children.

'My immediate ambition is to play in the Cámara des Deputados and hopefully to play in the Argentine Open one day. I played my first season as a professional in 2002. But I would also like to study to keep my mum happy!'

Alejandro 'Negro' Novillo-Astrada taking a tumble at the 2004 Gold Cup final, which his team, Azzurra, lost in a close match with Labegorce.

'The field was very dry the closer you got to the boards. Labegorce hit a backhander and I turned very fast to get the line. The ground was very hard there and my horse couldn't get a good grip, slipped and fell. When the horse fell, I was smashed against the boards and I can tell you that my muscles hurt for a whole week! The momentum of the fall took me over the boards, which was lucky in one way because it kept me clear of the falling horse.

'Being in the Queen's Cup final felt great though! I had never played the Queen's Cup and it is, after all, the second most important tournament in Europe. I was happy just to be part of it, yet I was also upset to have lost because I do think that we should have won.'

Luke Tomlinson riding Jethro, the gelding he won Best Pony on during the 2002 Queen's Cup final when playing for Emerging. Here he is marking Memo Gracida during the 2003 Cartier International Day when England beat Mexico.

'Having the job of marking Memo was the greatest thing and a wonderful opportunity. Unfortunately Memo wasn't as well mounted as he could have been and therefore he was not as difficult to mark as he might have been. Possibly the most difficult element to cope with in polo is when you are under-horsed. Jethro is not too easy to ride but he is one of my better horses.'

Memo Gracida praised the English team.

'I have to give credit to Luke and England, they played very well, especially Luke. They deserved the recognition. It's true that it is always difficult to play on borrowed horses as eighty per cent of polo is down to the horses. Make no mistake, the Tomlinson boys are third generation polo players; they work hard, are dedicated and always prepare well. Luke took the opportunity to mark me well. It was a good game although many things went against us, especially because Carlos injured his leg a few days before in the Gold Cup final. He was not, therefore, 100 per cent and as he is the pillar of our team it just didn't work out for us.'

Back view of Sebastian
Dawnay during the 2003
Queen's Cup semi-final match
against Oakland Park which
Labegorce won.

I took this shot on a
slower shutter speed than I
would use when I want to
achieve crisp sharp images.
The idea was to show the
power with which horses
push themselves forward. The
only point in focus is the tail
of Sebastian's horse.

Sebastian Dawnay, Black Bears, and Hissam Ali Hyder, Atlantic, during the 2004 Indian Empire Shield final.

This is an eighteen-goal tournament played at the end of May. Black Bears used it as a warm-up tournament and won it.

'Hissam Ali Hyder from Pakistan, a four-goal player was playing at number one. I played at four. The numbers one and four are often battling it out. I am defending and we are both waiting to see what is happening behind us. It is a complete struggle because if there is a pass coming, I have got to beat him and if he happens to beat me I get fired! We are both waiting in anticipation. Also, if the ball comes, Ali has to think because if I am going to win the ball he has to be quick as I am going to turn and attack.'

Lolo Castagnola, Dubai, using desperate measures against Juan Martin Nero, Azzurra, in the quarter-final match between Dubai and Azzurra, Queen's Cup 2004.

Azzurra were definitely the team to beat during the 2004 English high-goal season. Both times these two teams met, Azzurra came out on top.

'Azzurra played at a different level from the rest of the teams. They played like a twenty-six-goal team. Everybody else was on twenty-two goals! We didn't have much time in this match so we had to put as much pressure on our opponents as possible. We tried but we didn't manage it!'

Lolo Castagnola, la Dolfina, and Facundo Pieres, Ellerstina, coming at full blast towards the boards during the 2003 quarter-final at Palermo.

Lolo explains: 'It was quite a difficult match because at that stage in a tournament the loser is out! I will never forget this game because two of my horses got injured during the match. Fortunately they will be all right again but at the time it was quite a blow! They had to be out of action for four months. Here I am on Chino, an eight-year-old gelding I bought from Pancho Bensadon.'

(Right and opposite) Fernando 'Fati' Reynot-Blanco playing for Talandracas at the 2003 Gold Cup in Deauville.

Fernando explaines that his nickname 'Fati' was not given to him because he might have been a bit fat as a child but rather because his brother could not pronounce Fernando: 'He said Fati and it stuck!'

'We were not as good as we could have been that year. Team-mate Juan Martin was at that time already playing amazing polo! However, we lost a game we really shouldn't have lost, which, sadly, put us out of the final. But, that is polo!'

Fati has been a professional polo player for fourteen years.

'I became a professional polo player by chance because I was studying at the time but I got an invitation to come and play in France. This was the beginning of my career. When in Europe, I now mostly play in France. Other than that I live in Argentina. I also play in the US.'

Fati also played the Prince of Wales Cup in 1998. In Argentina he won the Copa Provincia in Buenos Aires, a twenty-eight goal tournament. In 1995 he won the Gold Cup in Sotogrande with La Palmeraie.

(Above and right) Celine Charloux playing at one for Loro Piana-Setteponti in the 2004 Gold Cup semi-final, Sotogrande.

Celine is the partner of Italian patron Alfio Marchini. Alfio entered two teams: he played for Loro Piana-Terranova and Celine teamed up with Juan Martin Nero, Gonzalito Pieres and Martin Espain in the Setteponti team.

Here Setteponti was battling for an entry into the final of the Gold Cup. However, Celine missed a few golden opportunities to score right at the start of the match. Scapa and Belgian patron Michael Redding proved to be too strong on the day.

'Having two Loro Piana teams in the competition was fun. We also hoped that we would end up playing against each other but it never happened!'

George Milford-Haven, patron
of Broncos during a league
match for the 2004
Warwickshire Cup against
Foxcote White.

George got into polo
thanks to his great-uncle
Lord Mountbatten who, after
the Second World War,
started playing polo with
Lord Cowdray.

'Lord Mountbatten
encouraged me to have a go
at polo and to take it up,
and so I started with Peter
Grace in 1982. I played high
goal in the late eighties. I
won the Queen's Cup, the
Gold Cup in Deauville and the
New Zealand Open. I then
stopped playing high goal for
a number of years and
started again in 2004 after
an absence of thirteen years.
Basically, the bank manager
stopped me from playing but,
fortunately, I managed to get
the green light again through
hard work! Now I would like
the Cowdray Gold Cup! It
probably takes four to five
years to do it and even then
there is no guarantee. It
takes a long time to get the
horsepower and the
infrastructure right, but I am
philosophical as well as
realistic about it. We have a
farm with 150 horses in
work about six miles from
Cowdray Polo Club; it is a
great set-up. My wife, Clare,
is also crazy about polo and
she sometimes plays for
Broncos instead of me.'

Hector Guerrero was brought in to replace the injured Piki Alberdi just one minute before the end of Larchmont's quarter-final match against Black Bears in the Queen's Cup 2004. Other than that, Hector played the season for Emerging.

'Piki got hit on the head and couldn't continue. I only touched the ball once and scored immediately! The game had almost been over though and Larchmont had already pratically won. I really didn't have to do much. Still, to score is always nice!'

Marcos Heguy, Azzurra, and Canadian Fred Mannix, Labegorce, engaged in a tough battle in front of the Royal Box in the 2004 Queen's Cup final. Carlos Gracida and Juan Martin Nero are not far behind the action.

Azzurra – the team all players rated the strongest that season – put up a real fight. Labegorce on the other hand were not going to let the final slip away a second time in a row after their narrow defeat by Dubai the year before. Carlos in particular was desperate to finally claim the Queen's Cup, a trophy that had eluded him up until 2004. Carlos thought of bringing Fred Mannix into the team and it was a decision that proved to have paid off!

'Carlos saw me during the US Open after a match he had just won of course! He wanted me to come and play with him for Labegorce. I had to ask my father first because the English season coincides with the Canadian season and my father wanted me to play the twenty-goal tournaments in Canada during July and August. I thought Carlos would not take me just for the Queen's Cup. Anyway, I spoke to my father more and told him that I really wanted to come, at least for the Queen's Cup. Also I thought that Luke was a very good player and I knew that Hubert organizes things the right way. He never cuts corners. I therefore knew we were going to be a good team with good horses. Fortunately my father agreed!'

Juan Martin Nero on the attack well in front of Lolo Castagnola,
Adolfo Cambiaso and Tariq Albwardi, on the way to victory in the
2004 Cowdray Gold Cup final.

'The final was a fantastic match! We never thought that we would
beat Dubai by such a big margin. Marcos was on fire and we just
played really well as a team. We only just lost the Queen's Cup final
and I think that during this final we just all played the best we had
played throughout the English season. Azzurra have very good horses.
They also proved to be very well organized. To keep the horses so
good for the duration of the season was a real achievement!

'Here I'm on the attack on one of the fastest horses I rode for
Azzurra. I had absolutely no problem passing Lolo!'

Juan Martin Nero kept his nose in front of Luke Tomlinson in the 2004 Queen's Cup final between Azzurra and Labegorce.

'I don't think we played very well in the final. Maybe we tapped the ball too much. I think that I certainly didn't hit the ball enough. I can't really remember that action. Maybe we had just made a mistake and I am trying to recoup the ball? The horse I am on is Eduardo Heguy's. In fact he lent me two of his best horses because I lost my best horse in the semis. This one is Lujan. A great horse! I am not sure if I didn't miss that ball, we were travelling so fast! I really think that we played better as a team in the semi-final!'

(Opposite) Azzurra and Geebung in a league match of the 2004 Veuve Cliquot Gold Cup. Although a few players are closely bundled together, Juan Martin Nero manages to hit the ball back.

'This match, the third one of the Gold Cup, was good and important for us. It was vital that we played well because we played really poorly in the first two matches. In that game we managed to turn our play around again. We succeeded in regaining confidence. We managed to play at the same level at which we had played the Queen's Cup. Maybe it took us two games to pick ourselves up from having lost the final of the Queen's Cup?'

Juan Martin Nero, Talandracas, and Pablo MacDonough, Oakland Park, neck and neck in the 2003 Ashton Cup final, a subsidiary of the Gold Cup.

Pablo travelled to England for the first time in 2001 where he only played the Gold Cup. In 2003 he was in England again just for the Gold Cup, replacing Gonzalito Pieres who had broken his finger earlier in the season. Pablo also played a full English season for Graff Capital in 2004.

'I enjoy playing with my brother Matias. I play a lot with him in Argentina where we play for Ellerstina. My father used to play. He was a four-goal player. He loves polo and breeds horses. I have played polo ever since I can remember anything about life! My most important goal is to win the Argentine Open with Ellerstina! I turned professional in 2002. Before that I used to study but I didn't finish. I wanted to concentrate fully on my polo. I feel that it is a privilege to be able to earn a living in a field I truly enjoy. Somehow, I couldn't really see myself sitting in an office for eight hours a day! Polo is a way of life. Any sportsman would say that his chosen field is his life but polo is not like football where after a match you have nothing else. Polo is different, you have horses; you can breed horses and, besides, it is fabulous to be in contact with another living being! Horses make up seventy per cent of the game. You can be a great player but if you don't have great horses you will never make it to the top!'

In this duel Juan Martin is riding Penelope a mare he sold to Edouard Carmignac, patron of Talandracas. 'On this occasion I just had more horsepower than Pablo!'

The Cartier Polo on Snow tournament celebrated its twentieth anniversary at the end of January 2004. Four teams: Cartier, Bank Hofmann, Maybach and Larchmont took part. Here Adriano Agosti, Cartier, and Juan Martin Nero, Larchmont, are in pursuit of the bouncing ball.

Jack Kidd, Larchmont, and
José Donoso, Cartier, St.
Moritz 2004.

José Donoso playing for the Cartier team during the twentieth St. Moritz polo tournament, January 2004.

'This 2004 tournament was the fourth time I had played in St. Moritz. I won it once and have played for the Cartier team on three occasions. For me it's the biggest show of polo after the Argentine Open. It's very glamorous, unique and very well organized. Playing at St. Moritz is also very special because it's by invitation only and, since they invite only a few, I feel very lucky to be amongst them! Playing on snow is very different from playing on grass; it's tougher and more physical for the players and horses, but the rules are the same. The conditions couldn't be more different though: it's very cold, it's windy and sometimes it even snows! Controlling the ball, especially when carrying it, is easier because it's bigger and lighter but, for the same reasons, the trajectory of the ball can be less accurate!'

(Opposite and left) Hernan Agote, playing for Maybach on snow at the twentieth anniversary of the St. Moritz tournament. Hernan is the older brother, by one year, of Alejandro Agote, who is also a polo player. The 2004 invitation was the third that Hernan had been given to play in St. Moritz.

'I am not a professional polo player like my brother. I work for the J.P. Morgan Bank. I love polo though and it's my hobby. I am very good friends with Mathias Gerrand-Hermès who kindly invites me to play in St. Moritz. Polo on snow is different: it's not as fast, but a lot of fun. St. Moritz is a top event; the organization is second to none, the atmosphere incredibly nice, and the facilities provided in the huge tent are just unbelievable! I always play for Maybach on horses that Mathias lends me. We lost by one goal to Larchmont. They did a good job thanks to Piki Alberdi and Juan Martin Nero, who are two great players!'

Hernan used to play a lot of polo before he went to high school in Philadelphia. Now he plays as much polo as he can fit in around his banking job.

'When you are young and single the lifestyle when playing polo is very nice but when you start having a family, it's not so good. I see this with my brother who travels for seven to eight months of the year. I am happy with my choice. I love polo, it is my favourite sport. I love breeding the horses and being outdoors, it's my hobby. Some people like to paint and sell their paintings, I like to breed and school the horses and sell them; I do this with my brother. He is the better player, the professional. It's true we look very much alike and people have a hard time telling as apart! I always tease Ale by saying that his handicap will be put down because people see me play and think that it's him!'

Eduardo Novillo-Astrada, Black Bears, and Luke Tomlinson, Emerging, taking a tumble during the 2002 Veuve Cliquot Gold Cup final. Fortunately neither players nor horses were any the worse for it. Both players explain what happened.

'I am on Grace, an Irish thoroughbred mare. She is probably one of the fastest horses I have. She was quite young at the time and her brakes were not very good then! I actually had the line and Eduardo saw me coming, yet I feel he crossed my line. Anyway, the umpires awarded a foul against me for crashing into him and gave a thirty yard penalty against us. Eduardo came off worse than me and I did apologize, which the umpires heard and I believe this to be the reason they awarded the foul against me. Neither Grace nor I got hurt. It was a touch scary at the time though!'

'As I remember it, the play changed. I was coming to get Milo. Suddenly the ball bounced and I got stuck in the middle. Luke couldn't stop and I got sandwiched. Fortunately nobody got hurt. It did scare me a bit though. It is not a situation one gets into everyday! I was rolling out so as not to get hurt. A penalty was given against Luke. I have had a few falls since, including a really bad one in Florida in 2004. It is part of the game and truthfully I don't ever think about the possible dangers.'

Eduardo Novillo-Astrada, Black Bears, and Pablo Spinacci,
Labegorce, playing a league match for the 2004 Gold Cup. The
match was played at Anningsley Park, home ground of
Labegorce.

That day Labegorce was unable to stop Black Bears'
continuous forward surge. Pablo Spinacci, playing at number
two, replaced Fred Mannix, who had commitments back in
Canada, for the duration of the Gold Cup. The day didn't go too
well for the home team. In the second half of the match Carlos
Gracida, who was suffering from an upset stomach, decided to
call it a day and called in Santiago Chavanne to replace him.

Chilean polo professional José Donoso playing for Cowdray, battling for the ball in front of the goalmouth during the 2003 Jack Gannon final, a subsidiary of the Gold Cup, Cowdray. Trying his best to prevent a goal is Guillermo Coutiño, Graff Capital.

'I believe I scored! I managed to hit the ball just a split second before I got hooked! It's a great photo because it's got the sticks and the ball, it gives a real sense of speed and seeing the goal post accentuates the drama of what is happening! I'm on Chusma, we were travelling flat out. Chusma is one of my best horses. She is an English thoroughbred and belongs to Mark Austin.'

Mauricio Devrient-Kidd is being hooked by Guillermo Coutiño in the 2003 final of the Jack Gannon Trophy, a subsidiary of the Gold Cup.

Mauricio, a professional polo player since the age of twenty, started his polo career in the USA and first came to play the English polo season in 1989 when the Argentines were allowed back after the Falklands war. Now based in England and Florida, Mauricio and his family enjoy the best of both worlds.

'Being hooked is very much part of polo. You first feel that someone has caught up with you. There is only a split second between the first of these photos and the last. At the point when you know that you have been caught, you have to think about your options. You can try to hit the ball even though you are going to get hooked, but should always be aware of whether or not a team-mate is behind you so that he can pick up the ball.

In this particular sequence I am delaying my shot as I know that I am going to get hooked, but the delay gives my team-mate a chance to catch up. He will then get the loose ball and take it through while I carry on my forward momentum. I might get the ball or might not but the aim is always to give my team-mate, who is coming from behind, a chance. The main objective is that the opposing team does not get the ball.

In this particular case, and as you can see in the last shot, neither of us got the ball! I am looking back to see where my team-mates are. Ideally, if you have a bit more time, you tap the ball. I could have tapped the ball to my nearside for example, ridden-off my opponent and hit the ball on my nearside. However Guillermo was already too close to me for that option. Don't forget all this is happening at full speed!'

José Donoso on the attack for Broncos in a 2004 Queen's Cup
league match, played at Cowdray. José is on his best mare
Baronesa, a Chilean thoroughbred.

'Baronesa has all the criteria of a great horse: she has a
lot of power, is very fast and handles well. Horses I play
should ideally handle well.

'A lot of things are happening for me in this picture. I'm
on my best horse and we are on the attack against Azzurra,
the best team of the 2004 season. Also, Marcos Heguy and
Juan Martin Nero, two great players, are in the picture too.
Baronesa is listening to me and enjoying the play!'

The Coronation Cup, also known as Cartier International Day, traditionally attracts a capacity crowd at Guards Polo Club. In 2004 the Chilean team, consisting of brothers Gabriel and José Donoso, Jaime Huidobro and Alejandro Vial, beat England. Henry Brett in his first year as captain, Luke and Mark Tomlinson and Will Lucas put their defeat down to a poor performance and felt that they should have been more disciplined.

José Donoso, here on board Gotera, was overjoyed by his team's success, particularly as this was the second time José, Gabriel and Jaime had won the Coronation Cup.

'Winning in 1998 and 2004 with my brother and Jaime, who is one of my best friends, means so much to me.

'I scored! I remember having had two very clear chances before that one that I mishit. But with this one I scored! I hit the ball a little wide on the approach shot but then managed to finish it off. The mare I am on comes from Chile. My brother Gabriel sold her to Nick Clarke who kindly lent her to me for the day.'

José Donoso has been a professional polo player since he finished high school. His desire to become a polo player goes back to his childhood.

'My father loved horses. He was a three-goal player and he gave us the opportunity to play polo. So, I have been surrounded by horses all my life really. Since my brother Gabriel was a polo player as well as being my idol, I never doubted my decision to try and make it in polo.'

José has won many tournaments and considers winning the under-twenty-one Open in Argentina to be one of his best memories. 'It meant a lot because it was my first ever visit to Palermo and I was very fortunate to be in a team with Adolfo Cambiaso, Sebastian Merlos and Lucas Criado!'

José has also won the Warwickshire Cup for Ellerstina when playing with Gonzalito Pieres. In Australia, José won the Melbourne Cup. Now his sight is firmly set on winning more high-goal matches in England.

'I'm still hoping, and working really hard, to win one of the two big ones in England!'

In this picture José is on Petitero, a stallion and embryo transplant from Argentina that used to belong to Gonzalito Pieres.

'Petitero is a fantastic horse. I love him! He is my nicest and most quiet horse.'

Marcos di Paola, Les Lions, giving it his all against Adolfo Cambiaso in the 2004 Veuve Cliquot quarter-final.

Marcos was absolutely outstanding on the day, scoring some amazing goals. Polo followers and players thought that this match was the best match of the entire tournament, with the final result being, Dubai beat Les Lions 12–10.

'I was feeling very well and very relaxed that day. We played Dubai the way we had to play them and it almost worked! Cambiaso was coming up my left-hand side and it was one of those days when I felt that I could possibly overtake him. So I just went for it and a couple of times it worked which was really great! I was very pleased with my horse Colorado. He is an Argentine-bred gelding that I brought over to England this season. I didn't know him very well at first but now I do! It was amazing to feel how much he had improved during the season.'

Chilean Gabriel Donoso has
been a professional polo
player since 1982. In
England, Gabriel won the
Queen's Cup in 1988 and the
Cowdray Gold Cup in 1993. In
France, he won the Deauville
Gold Cup on three occasions.

'The sweetest victory
must be when we won the
1993 Gold Cup in England
beating Ellerston Black who
were the strongest team at
the time. The match went
into eight chukkas: two
overtime chukkas. Polo
means everything to me! I
enjoy being part of a team,
and if you ask me about my
strong points they would
have to be being a good
team player and allowing my
team-mates to shine. I am
not selfish and I don't mind
if I don't appear to be the
best player on the field. I
like contributing to my
team's win.'

In this picture Gabriel is
playing for Salkeld against
Black Bears in a league
match for the 2004
Warwickshire Cup.

Adolfo Cambiaso, Dubai, and Marcos Heguy,
Azzurra, fighting for a bouncing ball during
the 2004 Veuve Cliquot Gold Cup final.

Although Dubai started off well and led
by three goals to zero early on in the
match, Azzurra came back with a vengeance
and almost blew Dubai off the field.

The Dubai team were united in
acknowledging that Azzurra was not only
the strongest team of the 2004 season but
was also on fire the day of the final.

'Azzurra was more like a twenty-six-goal
team in a twenty-two-goal tournament!'

**Adolfo Cambiaso, La Dolfina, and Mariano Aguerre, Indios
Chapaleufu I, at the knockout stages in Palermo 2003.**

**Cambiaso reaches for balls other players would only
dream of being able to reach!**

**'When I reach for the ball I don't think, I just do it! All I
try to do is to anticipate the other player's move or thought
and to just be that little fraction ahead. I try to outsmart
my opponents.'**

Marcos Heguy on Suerte, one of his best horses, in the 2003 Gold Cup in Deauville.

This had been the fourth year Marcos played in the Gold Cup for André Fabre's team, Royal Barriere. They won it in 2001 and 2002. This time they reached the final yet again but lost to HB.

'The ground was a bit of a problem in Deauville. It was very deep which made it difficult for the horses and for hitting the ball because the ball often got buried in the divots! HB beat us because we didn't make the most of the horsepower we actually had. That, again, was due to the poor quality of the field. It was rather broken up which made for much slower play. Our horsepower couldn't give us the advantage it should have. But the organizers promised to address the problem of the fields for the coming year's tournament.'

Marcos has been a ten-goal player since 1987. His victories are countless. His special memories are, however, linked with winning the Argentine Open six times.

'For a polo player, the Argentine Open represents the greatest tournament of our sport. It is really important to compete in it. It must be every polo player's dream and ambition to compete in it. As for polo, well it's simply a fantastic sport. because I love horses; I have a special passion for them. To be involved with horses, to breed them and everything that goes with it, as well as the game itself, makes polo a complete sport for me.'

Brothers Marcos and Bautista Heguy played against each other in the 2004 semi-final of the Veuve Cliquot Gold Cup. Bautista and the Larchmont team gave Azzurra a really good match. However, team-mates Piki Alberdi, Ryan Pemble and patron Marek Dochnal couldn't quite pull it off. Azzurra won by just one goal, 10–9.

The 2004 season was Larchmont's first high-goal season and, as Bautista points out, 'One thing is for sure, Marek is learning!'

'It is also my first year playing with Piki, we have actually never played together before. We do get along very well. My feeling after our first league match at Guards was that we might already have a chance of making it to the semis of both the Queen's and the Gold Cup. With a bit of luck we could even have won a cup. Of course it was our first season and we have to get better horses for the four-goal player. Marek, however, is committed to building the team for years to come. So, my feeling remains, winning one of the big ones will happen in the future! I think that Marek is a really nice guy. I really would like us to win for him, because he is doing everything the right way.'

Pite Merlos, La Dolfina, is going for the ball while
Miguel Novillo-Astrada, La Aguada, is keeping him in
check during the 2003 Argentine Open.

La Dolfina had kept a nose in front in every
chukka up until the seventh when La Aguada
managed to level the score at nine all. The final
chukka belonged to La Aguada. Miguel played terrific
polo, and Javier converted a corner which took the
brothers ahead before Ignacio put the ball through
the posts twice more. The final score was 12–10.

'Pite is a very good, clever player. He is very
good with the ball. He usually tries to keep his
team around him and to conserve the position of
the ball.'

Sebastian Dawnay, Ireland, and Spain's Pascual Sainz de Vicuña battling for the ball during their 2003 European Championships league match.

Sebastian Dawnay: 'I remember the Spanish team being very good! Pascual is always going for it! Spain won the league match but we met them again in the match for third place and pulled it off then!'

Pascual Sainz de Vicuña: 'I had a lot of fun playing the European Championships, especially as this had been my first time playing for Spain outside Spain or Argentina. I played at one. It's a position where you have to be very fast and it helps if you are skilful with the ball. I love playing with the ball, and so it's a position I enjoy a lot. Also it's natural for me to play forward. I have to learn more about playing the man though!

'I would love to play the Queen's Cup or the Gold Cup one day! I think that the English polo season is one of the best, very competitive, and so hopefully I will play in England again one day!'

Ireland and Spain met again in the match for third and fourth place during the 2003 European Championships held at Dallas Burston. The two teams had just turned at the same time and were charging towards the ball.

Sebastian Dawnay and Pascual Sainz de Vicuña remember the match.

'I was still recovering from an injury to my shoulder and my shoulder was actually strapped together. I could hardly steer! I was in constant pain. It was also fun to be playing with my cousin Charles Beresford especially as we had never played in the same team before!'

'Right at the beginning of the match one of our players got injured and we could only replace him with an Argentine player, which in actual fact was not allowed. So, although we finished the match we had effectively already lost. Ireland won!'

Bautista Heguy, Indios Chapaleufu I, in the 2003 semi-final of the Argentine Open in Palermo, which La Dolfina won. Bautista has, however, won the Open five times with Indios Chapaleufu I. In the picture opposite he is reaching for a nearside forehand just ahead of Lolo Castagnola, and in the photo below, Bautista is riding-off Sebastian Merlos.

'Playing the Palermo Open is the top for every high-goal player! It is the best tournament in the world because the level of play is extremely high. It's great to play in front of a crowd of 20,000 people who all know the game inside out. It compares to playing in front of a knowledgeable football crowd. It is a completely different feeling from that felt when playing in England. In Palermo I get more nervous but I like nervous tension. Also, I like playing with my brothers. Every year when November comes round and Palermo begins it is something I really look forward to. And, although I have been playing in Palermo for fifteen years, when I go out there to stick and ball for the first match, it really is special! No matter how often one has won the open it's always a tournament every player wants to win over and over again.'

Bautista reached his ten-goal handicap when he was twenty. Now in his early thirties, he thinks that he was too young to really give a huge amount of meaning to having reached the highest distinction.

'I didn't realize the importance of it. Perhaps also because I was put from eight immediately to ten. To tell you the truth, I never think of my handicap. I just try to improve my game of polo and to be a good team-mate. You can never think that you are a great player. You have to constantly try to improve your game. At the end of each match I am conscious of the mistakes I have made and I will try not to make those same mistakes again. No two games are ever the same and every match makes you think. To be a good polo player you have to use your mind. It's not only about hitting the ball and scoring penalties. Sometimes you might not impress the crowds but you are playing well because you are taking an opponent out or opening a gap for your team-mate to score. Yes, the goal scorer might take all the applause and yet a team-mate played a huge part in it. I always say that it is important to realize that you have scored a goal because of great teamwork. So, it is important to learn that you cannot do it alone! As soon as you believe that you can do it alone you are no longer a good polo player.'

Sebastian is just as passionate about Palermo! He and his brother Pite played for La Dolfina from 2000 until 2003. Together they won the Open in 2002.

'I remember the match against Chapaleufu I very well. It was a tense match. All semi-finals usually are, because both teams really want to reach the final. When La Dolfina plays it is always a nice match to watch; La Dolfina plays an open play in which there are actually not many bumps or fouls. We always have fun. Palermo is a tournament where you really challenge yourself and push yourself to the limit. You play with the best and against the best, and to perform at that level is great.'

In 2004 three Merlos brothers: Pite, Sebastian and their youngest brother Agustin, were playing as La Mariana.

'It's the name of the polo club my father built. It is also the name of my grandmother, my mother's mother. Sadly I never met my grandmother because she died when my mother was eighteen. The last time we played as La Mariana, we reached the final of Palermo but lost to Chapaleufu I: all the Heguys. So we are hoping to go one better this year!'

Paco de Narvaez an eight-goal player will be accompanying the three brothers.

Juan Ignacio 'Pite' Merlos
playing for La Dolfina during
the 2003 Argentine Open.

'The quarter-finals of the
2003 Open against Ellerstina
was a very close match.
Ellerstina was the youngest
team in the competition,
they had great quality
players and were very
competitive. They were very
well organized and gave us
reason to worry at the
beginning of the match, but
fortunately it worked out
well and in our favour at the
end. When playing the Open
you get a feeling of being
alive!

'As a polo player you are
always looking forward to
the next Palermo. No matter
what pains you have, what
age you are and what team
you are playing with. The
crème de la crème are there

competing. There is so much talent and speed in Palermo.

'For me polo represents two things: there is the horse breeding, and I am so into breeding, it is
so unpredictable and difficult; the second thing is my desire to, hopefully, give my son the love of
horses and the love of polo because it offers such a wonderful life.'

Pite, the older brother by four years, and Sebastian Merlos had teamed up with Adolfo
Cambiaso and Lolo Castagnola from 2000 until 2003. Together they won the Hurlingham in 2001,
and the Hurlingham plus the Argentine Open in 2002. The two brothers started their professional
polo career when playing for Urs Schwarzenbach and Black Bears. They played together from 1991
to 1996.

'Everything I am in polo now I owe to Urs and Francesca Schwarzenbach. Urs was the first
patron who believed in me and who put all his trust in my ability. He made me the captain of his
team when I was only twenty years old. I have only the fondest words of appreciation for Urs and
Francesca. Together we won the Queen's Cup twice, the Gold Cup once, the Warwickshire Cup three
times, and the Ellerston Gold Cup twice. I have so many good memories from these days.'

Sebastian Merlos in the 2004 US Open quarter-finals.

'The US Open is very special to me. I played my first tournament as a professional there in 1990. I won the US Open with Memo Gracida and my brother Pite that year, so one can say it was a great start to my career. I went from a being a four-goal player straight to seven goals after that win. I also won the US Open in 1995 and 1998.'

Sebastian also won the Argentine Open in 2002 and played in the final five times. His other successes came when he was playing with his brother Pite for Black Bears.

'We won a lot with Black Bears! Playing with Urs was fantastic. I felt like being another member of the Schwarzenbach family. What Urs and Pite built was amazing. That era from 1991 to 1996 was a big moment in polo. Black Bears were always neck and neck with Ellerston White. We had great matches.'

Matt Lodder, Dubai, pushing hard to try to put off Mark Tomlinson, Graff Capital, from making contact with the ball during the 2004 Gold Cup semi-final, Cowdray.

Matt has ridden all his life. He first played for Dubai in 2003. Although Matt was working with Adolfo Cambiaso in 2004, he was only brought into the team for the Gold Cup tournament. Dubai won the match against Graff Capital 17–12.

'I was a bit rusty at the beginning of the Gold Cup, but it went well. Adolfo must like me because he asked me to come over to Argentina to work for him at the end of the 2003 season, and I am still working for Adolfo in England. Before the Gold Cup I was bringing on his horses in medium-goal tournaments.'

Matt Lodder, Dubai, and Ernesto Trotz, Les Lions, in the 2004 Gold Cup quarter-final, Cowdray.

It was a tough match because Les Lions looked really strong. Dubai being Dubai, however, managed to secure their entry into the semi-final by eventually winning 12–10.

Here the two players are galloping at full speed, the ball being only a few yards ahead of them.

'We were travelling at quite a speed up the field towards the goal. I was trying my hardest to prevent Ernesto from reaching the ball, taking it further up and scoring.'

Rick McCarthy on the attack
playing for patron Ron
Wanless's Wastecorp team
against Ellerston at the 2004
J.D. Macleod Cup final.

'Reaching the final at
Ellerston was like fulfilling my
childhood dream. When I was
about twelve I was a
spectator at Ellerston to
watch a forty-goal invitation
match. I shook hands with
Kerry Packer, and got his
autograph! From that moment
on I was hooked on polo.

'Here I'm on Ice, a mare I
bought as a four-year-old off
the racetrack and trained. She
was very difficult to train.
Retraining is always more
difficult. Basically you have to
teach ex-racehorses to turn,
to stop, to relax and not to
run off! To get her as far as
being able to play her at
Ellerston was a great
achievement. In the final I
played her in two chukkas.'

Australian duo Rick McCarthy, Wastecorp, and Mike King, patron of Elysian Fields, in a league match for the 2004 J.D. Macleod Cup, Ellerston.

Mike is on Bonus, 'A little horse that tries really hard!'

'This was a closely disputed match. We only just won by one goal. What I like most about polo is the opportunity to ride really good horses and to travel the world.'

Mike plays mostly in Australia and New Zealand and has travelled to England where he has played medium goal, an experience he really enjoyed.

Rick grew up on a farm and has always been around horses. He loved polo the minute he was introduced to it. Rick also loves training horses with a view to selling them on.

'I love the speed as well as the horse's athleticism. I wasn't very good at polo to begin with but I have always been able to get a tune out of horses. Now I am constantly in pursuit of perfection. For me the beauty of polo lies in the fact that a little country boy from a small rural farming area in New South Wales can be playing polo against an affluent businessman like Mike King. In polo there are no barriers, which makes it so very special.'

Commenting on Rick, his father Chris says, 'Rick took to the game like a duck to water. He played most of his better polo when playing for Garangula. At school he was a rugby player and he is a rugby player in polo too!'

Tom Morley and Adolfo
Cambiaso in the closely
disputed 2004 Gold Cup
quarter-final match between
Les Lions and Dubai, Cowdray.

This was Tom Morley's
first time playing for Les
Lions.

'Les Lions was a nice team
with great players like
Ernesto Trotz and Marcos di
Paola. They made playing
with them really easy. The
quarter-final was the best
match of the 2004 Gold Cup;
everybody was on the edge of
their seats. At the end we
lost by two goals but we
were down by one or drawing
all along until the last
minute of the last chukka!
This was a tight battling
shot. When playing against
Adolfo, you have to think of
him as just another man on a
horse but, at the end of the
day, he is amazing. It is
difficult to get close to him
and I am surprised I got that
close! He must have gone the
wrong way by accident!'

Bautista Heguy playing for Cadenza in the 2003 Queen's Cup.

Bautista has been coming to England for fifteen years and has only missed playing the English season twice because of a contract in Brunei. He has won the Queen's Cup twice: once with Ellerston and once with Givan.

'I always say that I enjoy winning the Queen's Cup more than winning the Gold Cup. I love playing here at Guards, maybe because of the Queen?'

HRH Prince Charles during the 2004 Charity Match for the Prince's Trust, Cowdray. Jack Kidd, playing for Audi, is attempting to put the Prince under pressure.

Guards Polo Club, 2003.

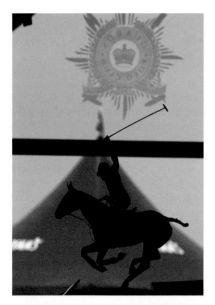

HRH Prince Harry during the 2003 Gulf Co-Operation Council Day in aid of the Prince's Trust at Guards Polo Club. Prince Harry, playing at one for the Prince of Wales's team about to reach the ball just ahead of Gaston Laulhe, GCC team.

Prince William,
Cirencester Polo Club,
2003.

On June 26th 2004, HM the
Sultan of Brunei put in a
rare appearance in England
when he teamed up with
HRH Prince William, John
Smail and HRH the Prince of
Wales for the Dorchester
Polo Trophy: a charity match
between Highgrove and
Lovelocks in aid of The
British Wheelchair Sports
Foundation and Sue Ryder
Care Charity. It was only a
shame that the weather
gods had not been kinder
on the day. In fact it had
easily been the wettest day
of the summer!

A FAMILY AFFAIR

When I was getting ready to start work on this book, and was looking through the list of polo players entered in various teams, I noticed that most surnames popped up more than once. Sometimes the same family names would appear in the same team, and on other occasions would be present on another patron's list of players. Usually, although not necessarily, those related players were even competing for the same trophy. At other times they were competing in tournaments of different levels or in tournaments that might be held concurrently, like Deauville and Sotogrande.

It soon became apparent that having the same surname didn't inevitably mean that the players were brothers: some were cousins. A newcomer to the game might be forgiven for feeling a touch confused by it all, but I determined to, firstly, not let it confuse me and to, secondly, get to the bottom of it. I did not, however, go as far as acquiring family trees of various polo-playing clans! But it was not destined to be that simple. When discussing this phenomena with a family member, the situation would either be clarified immediately or confound me more.

While showing a player a picture I was going to use in the book, I might ask him something about another player who was featured in the same shot. Suddenly the word 'cousin' would come up again,

and, intrigued, I would make a mental note not to make the same mistake of identity when speaking to the cousin in question!

To illustrate my point, let's look at the name 'Heguy', a very familiar and popular name in polo circles. Bautista, Marcos and Horacio Heguy are brothers. Alberto (also known as Pepe), Eduardo (nicknamed Ruso) and Ignacio (also known as Nachi) Heguy are also brothers, and cousins of the three Heguys above! There will, of course, be no confusion if you know that they are the children of the two great polo-playing brothers of the 1960s and seventies: the first set of brothers are Horacio Heguy's sons and the second set are the sons of Alberto Pedro Heguy. Just to trip up newcomers to polo again, however, there are those polo-playing cousins who do not share the same name, such as Simon Keyte and John Paul Clarkin. The Argentine players Gonzalito Pieres and the MacDonough brothers, Matias and Pablo, are also cousins.

In England the well-known Tomlinson brothers, Luke and Mark, and their sister Emma, are the cousins of Will Lucas. Will's father and Claire Tomlinson are brother and sister.

Interestingly, patrons like employing brothers or cousins in their teams. For example, Markus Graff, patron of Graff Capital, told me that he wanted to

Javier Novillo-Astrada in the 2003 Argentine Open semi-final, a match the Novillo-Astrada brothers' team, La Aguada, won by beating Indios Chapaleufu I 11–8. The Indios team comprised Marcos Heguy, Bautista Heguy, Horacio Heguy and Mariano Aguerre.

'The Heguys are always tough to beat. We played really well. We were in control during the last chukka and pulled it off! Semi-finals are always tough! Mariano Aguerre was in front of me and I was about eighty yards from goal. When Bautista checked a little bit, he made room for me and I had a chance to take a swing at the ball. I was lucky enough for the ball to go in! It was also just in time before the end of the chukka.'

play the 2004 English high-goal season with Matias MacDonough because he got along well with Matias, an eight-goal player, when playing in Gstaad. As soon as he found out that Matias's brother Pablo, also an eight-goal player, was available as well, Markus jumped at the chance of signing up both brothers because he knew that it would heighten his team's chances considerably. Joining the team for the season was six-goal player Mark Tomlinson who confirmed that a team that musters siblings is a very strong team because brothers have a great understanding of each others' game which, in turn, generates a huge advantage.

A patron will always try to sign up players who are close to one another because the chances of brothers or cousins getting along well are fairly good. Furthermore, rivalry amongst brothers doesn't really arise within a polo team. Every player has a well-defined strategic job to do and each player will try to fulfil his role to the best of his ability and conduct his play with the team's interest at heart.

Players themselves always point out that playing polo with their siblings or relatives adds another dimension to the enjoyment of the game. And, what is very apparent is that patrons and players alike want to play polo in a pleasant atmosphere in the company of people they like being with.

It should, therefore, not come as much of a surprise that, throughout the history of polo, successful teams have very often been made up of brothers or cousins. This statistic applies to high-goal polo throughout the world and is most apparent in Argentina. The most famous example being the Harriott/Heguy combination who represented the Coronel Suárez Polo Club and won the Argentine Open a record twelve times, six of those in consecutive years from 1974 through to 1979.

But there are, of course, some exceptions to that 'family' rule and one can find great players who neither come from a polo-playing dynasty nor have any siblings in the sport. These players would be the first to admit that 'going solo' in polo is difficult.

Henry Brett, the newly appointed 2004 captain of the English polo team, is one such player. Despite the fact that Henry acknowledges that doing it on your own is much tougher, his determination and talent have still propelled him to being the highest-handicapped English player at present.

Argentine superstar Adolfo Cambiaso and Bartolome 'Lolo' Castagnola are two other examples. Adolfo is only too aware of the difficulty of 'trying to make it on your own in polo'. Fortunately, he and Lolo started playing polo at the same time and because they found themselves alone and in the same predicament, they became the best of friends. Adolfo believes that in order to grow and get better in polo 'you have to be at least a couple of brothers or cousins'. Adolfo even goes as far as saying, 'on your own you get nowhere'. Lolo and Adolfo are now brothers-in-law, and so my advice would be to watch out for the next generation they will produce. Cousins!

As families have such an obvious influence on successful polo, it was important for me to study some polo-playing families in detail. I was spoilt for choice but decided to narrow the field by concentrating on two sets of male siblings.

Because of their recent successes, I decided to take a closer look at the English brothers, Luke and Mark Tomlinson, winners of the 2003 Cowdray Gold Cup. And, to include the Argentine perspective, the phenomenal success the Novillo-Astradas had had during the 2003 Argentine season led me straight to the five highly motivated brothers.

My apologies to the countless other successful siblings in polo, but many of them are featured in the Polo in Action sections.

The Tomlinson Brothers

Luke and Mark Tomlinson, brothers with the hottest polo pedigree in England, have not only won big tournaments individually when playing for well-known patrons, but have also scooped England's most sought-after polo cup when pairing up with Nina Vestey and John Paul 'JP' Clarkin for Hildon Sport during the 2003 high-goal polo season. Never before had English brothers together with a lady player won the Gold Cup at Cowdray.

Luke, born on 27th January 1977 (the older brother by five years), and Mark both put their interest in polo down to having been introduced to the sport at a very early age, which if you happen to have been born into a well-established polo-playing family seems inevitable.

Mother, Claire Tomlinson, née Lucas, an excellent polo player and at five goals the highest-

Brothers Mark and Luke Tomlinson with the Gold Cup trophy they won with friends Nina Vestey and JP Clarkin in 2003.

On seeing this photo, Mark (the younger by five years) said that it underlines the respect he has for Luke as an older brother. 'Luke means a lot to me as a brother and team-mate.' Luke pointed out that Mark is a great polo player, a great person and someone who strikes a great balance between commitment and having a good time. 'I really love playing with Mark primarily because we complement each other so well on the polo field.'

rated lady player during her era, has been most influential in nurturing the brothers' development and progress. Not only is she in demand as a polo coach today, she was also the polo coach for the Beaufort Pony Club when her children were young. Father, Simon Tomlinson, is just as important to the family set-up. He played polo for the army as well as teaming up with Claire. Together they won a considerable number of tournaments, notably the Queen's Cup in 1982. Simon also coaches. During the 2003 European Championships held at Dallas Burston he helped the German polo team. Both parents take an immense interest in their children's careers, which at times can lead to quite a busy lifestyle! While Luke might be playing in

Luke Tomlinson and Jaime Huidobro neck and neck during the 2004 Coronation Cup at Guards, with Chile playing England.

Chile won the battle and this was Luke's comment on the match.

'We played pretty badly. We were less disciplined than the Chileans; we really should have been more disciplined! Also, we should have been better mounted in the middle chukkas.'

Sotogrande, Mark could be entered in Deauville. Added to that, their daughter Emma, the eldest of the three, will, time permitting, also be playing somewhere. Emma is a busy vet but still very much a part of the family operation. She has the first, and so far only, embryo transplant station in England. The family run the Beaufort Polo Club and numerous polo tournaments from their beautiful farm in Gloucestershire; they also have a farm in Argentina and spend the Argentine polo season there which helps the boys' careers. Emma has started to build up her reputation as a vet in Argentina and also enjoys playing there.

As a youngster, Luke recalls he was not too keen on horses initially. He remembers going through a phase aged five and six when he gave up riding. 'We

were made to work quite hard in the stables and I preferred my bicycle. I could just throw it in a corner. No mucking out needed there!' He even went as far as saving up for a small motorbike. But after he broke his leg riding it, Luke decided, 'Being around horses was not so difficult after all, and my parents got me back into it through hunting.'

Luke was by no means pushed into becoming a professional polo player. His father actually discouraged him at one stage because in his era, the 1980s, 'polo wasn't very professional'. Luke could have done whatever he wanted to do but, 'Polo was there and it was beginning to be fun too, so, going into polo became a natural progression.'

Luke's first love was, however, hunting. A few years back he whipped-in for the Beaufort and it did cross Luke's mind, quite seriously at one point, that he might go into hunting full time. 'I wanted to hunt a pack of hounds and be a master/huntsman.'

Nonetheless, at present Luke is very committed to polo. His only concern being that living as a professional polo player is a very unstable job. 'It is rather difficult to be on the market every year looking for a job, compared to working in the city where people work for the same firm, never having to look further then their first job.'

Well, there is a price to pay for everything in life and although Luke strikes me as being a person who needs stability in his life, his love for horses and passion for polo have, fortunately for those of us who enjoy his play, won on this occasion. He says that because polo is run on a handicap system it can

In August 2004 Mark played
in the Sotogrande Gold Cup
tournament. Here he is on
Rizzo being followed by
Marcos di Paola.

Italian patron Alfio
Marchini had two Loro Piana
teams in Sotogrande. Mark
played for Loro Piana-
Terranova together with Alfio,
Milo Fernandez-Araujo and
Gonzalo Bordieu. In this
match they lost to Scapa yet
went on to win the
subsidiary final.

be very contradictory. 'You could be playing very
well and be put up by one goal and yet you could be
out of a job for the following season because you
don't fit the bill anymore. This side of polo can, if I
let it, play with my head a lot.'

A good example of this is that Mark went up by
a goal after their Gold Cup victory which meant
that the four could not defend their title in 2004.

Nevertheless Luke did not go empty-handed
during the 2004 season. Carlos Gracida, asked Luke
to join the Labegorce team because, as Carlos put it,
'Luke beat me in three out of four important
matches! Besides, I always thought he was a good
player. One that I'd rather have on my side than
playing against me.'

Carlos's strategy paid off. Luke's hard work in

Luke on Santos during the
2004 Gold Cup final.

'We all played really well
on the day, but we were
really lucky too because
technically Azzurra was
better than us! Realistically
Azzurra is a twenty-six-goal
team! We also went up by
two goals: Carlos played
really well and went up to
ten after the Queen's Cup;
Fred Mannix went up to
seven. I was really happy to
have won. It was a brilliant
match. Azzurra was such a
good team and to have
beaten them was brilliant!'

defence contributed greatly to Labegorce winning the splendid Queen's Cup: a trophy Luke had previously won with Emerging in 2002 but one that had eluded the Mexican player until 2004.

Luke was obviously very happy to have been picked by Gracida, especially as in Luke's eyes, 'Carlos is the world's best player ever! He has won the Argentine Open playing at one and at four and the US Open playing at two and three. As for the Cowdray Gold Cup, he won it eleven times!' Further, he insists that Carlos is an amazing team player and

Mark on Chico during the 2003 Challenge Cup final played at Cowdray two weeks after the Gold Cup final.

Mark was playing with his mother Claire, his cousin Will Lucas and Satnam Dhillon for Los Locos against the Vampire Bats, a team local to the Beaufort.

'I felt really good that day. I scored the best goal ever! It's a great tournament to win. I really enjoy playing with Mum. It is so very satisfying because she puts so much into our polo. She has come down from handicap five to two now because she spends a lot of time coaching.'

'At the end of the day, polo is a team sport and that is an aspect of the game that I enjoy most.'

Luke considers two of his own strengths in polo to be his defensive play and his string of horses. He trains his horses himself but gets much-appreciated help from mother, Claire. 'I listen to Mum a lot. She is an amazing horsewoman. She will make a horse do all sorts of things!'

Luke likes watching all good players. He names in particular, Miguel Novillo-Astrada and Milo

Fernandez-Araujo and says that he tries to 'take something from each of them'. Milo, however, has played a big role in moulding Luke's game, which is no surprise as he had played for Luke's parents for six seasons during Luke's most formative years. 'Milo is like a brother to me, a great influence and a bit of a mentor.'

Like so many other polo professionals, Luke agrees that playing polo is a passion, but he points out, 'To be able to feed this passion you need horses which is by far the most difficult part to achieve and maintain.'

Mental strength is another facet on which Luke puts a lot of emphasis. 'I'd be inclined to say that it's all in the head. Just as you can get horses that work fine in training and become nervy and behave differently as soon as you play them, so can players.' Luke tries to work hard on building his mental strength and keeping his nerves at bay. 'The more I want to win the more I tend to get nervous. Psychologically it gets very interesting because I believe that if you purely concentrate on playing well and forget that you want to win, winning will come as a natural progression. The worst thing one can do is to be constantly looking at the scoreboard.'

As for Luke's ball control, well, he modestly declares that he has never been blessed with great ball skills but that he considers himself good on a horse, not before stating that he could improve in this area too. He justifies this remark. 'A really good horseman can get on any horse and, more importantly, make any horse do exactly what he

(Left) Mark during the 2003 Veuve Cliquot Gold Cup final in great harmony with Rizzo.

Mark plays a lot of geldings and believes that geldings have more heart than mares.

'They have more staying power. A mare might tell you where to go after four, five minutes play. In top polo you have to have a machine and by that I mean that a horse has to be able to do everything. Run, stop, turn and, most importantly, it should be able to do these things with ease. The first thing I look for in a horse is that it is relaxed when I take it out for a canter.'

(Above) Luke in the 2003 Gold Cup semi-final when Hildon Sport beat Dubai.

'I think that we were always going to win. Cambiaso having a bad elbow helped a bit too! Also I think that their horses were slightly more tired than ours. I feel that we dominated the match. However, Dubai is always a very dangerous team. They only need the ball for one minute in a chukka to score three goals! If you miss opportunities and give the ball away, you are bound to lose to Dubai.'

wants. And, more remarkably, the horses would stay calm while things are being asked of them. I don't think that my horse skills match up to that although I'd like them to…one day.'

In my view Luke is being very modest about his horsemanship because he also discloses that he neither likes to exhaust his horses and run them flat out unless he is sure that the run counts, nor to stop

Luke Tomlinson, Jaipur, giving it his all in a ride-off against Lolo Castagnola, Tradition, during the 2004 Sotogrande Gold Cup semi-final.

'When playing against Lolo you have to give as good as you get!'

his horses harder than they have to be stopped. 'It's like out hunting, I mean I love jumping but if I see an open gate I will always favour that route, especially as there will surely be a hedge round the corner that you will have to jump because you can't get around it.' Undoubtedly horses last longer this way, and applying this attitude to the polo field 'makes a player think quicker, often a few plays ahead and', so Luke thinks, 'it probably also makes

one a better player'. Isn't this a clear sign of being a good horseman?

Futhermore, Luke enjoys going to the stables to chat with his horses but he tries not to get too attached to them. 'Losing one of my best mares when playing for Emerging left me feeling devastated.'

It strikes me that Luke is a very sensitive, self-analytical, hard-working and methodical person and, fortunately, he also remembers the moments when, in his eyes, he did ride a horse well, when he did hit a backhand well or when he made an immaculate pass. He confirms: 'These are the moments when the saying "the more you practise the luckier you get" makes sense, and when a little thing inside me goes click and makes it all worthwhile.'

Despite his worries about the instability of the job, I am sure Luke would not want to swap his job for one where he would be bent over a desk. Not with his height, anyway! Besides, Luke loves playing with his brother Mark.

The five years that separate the Tomlinson brothers do, from Mark's point of view, mean that they do not do everything together and that they like doing their own things. Both would agree that they have very different characters. When they play on the same team this is, however, a big asset for polo as the two brothers and their different styles complement each other so well.

When speaking to Mark one can't help but remark on his fantastic enthusiasm for the sport and how multi-talented he is. As Luke puts it: 'Mark will try to do everything and most likely do it all well!'

Born on 25th March 1982, Mark bubbles over with an unequivocal and almost immeasurable sparkle, comparable to nature's energies at the outset of spring. On the polo field this translates into Mark's unforgettable and impressive controlled forward-surging aggression. Mark usually plays at two, running forward and always ready to score.

Most of all, Mark simply loves speed and he knows that when he is drawn against tough players he also has to get stuck into the ride-offs. He does, however, concede that he wouldn't go as far as saying that he truly enjoys 'having to give a very physical player as good as he gets'.

For Mark, getting into polo was almost a forgone conclusion. He remembers picking up a stick when he was four and having his first game at the age of seven. Being the youngest it was pretty evident that Mark would be emulating his siblings particularly as it was also the era when his parents were notably active players. When Mark was young he didn't think much about what he was doing, he just did it because everybody around him was doing it. 'But once I was old enough to think about what I was getting into, I realized how much I was actually enjoying it.'

Mark started playing polo competitively at the age of ten and soon found out how much he enjoyed competition. Until he was sixteen Mark played polo for the Beaufort Pony Club during the summer months and competed in hunter trials during the winter months. Mark also had a pony he

used for show jumping and eventing but because the same pony was also used for polo, he admits that his dressage let him down! The decision to move into polo full time was, therefore, pretty much made for him and, besides, his natural talent for the sport is obvious to everyone. As Mark points out, 'Having practically been breast-fed on polo has probably got

Luke playing his mare Grace for Labegorce and eyeing up the ball ready to unleash his mallet for a backhand.

'We played well that day against Emerging and, by winning, we reached the final of the Jack Gannon Cup, a subsidiary of the Gold Cup.'

Mark in full swing on Chico during the 2003 Gold Cup final.

'For me polo is a unique sport involving two skills. One being hand/eye coordination, the other, speed! It sends out a huge rush of adrenaline because it's such a fast and furious game. I find it gets very addictive and difficult to get away from. I love the competitiveness, winning and working out the process of how you are going to win. The horse management and training is hard work. But it's the end result and the prospect of winning that spurs me on.'

something to do with it!'

Nonetheless, Mark does work hard at his game and acknowledges that his mother was the first one to help and has been extremely influential right through his career. 'This doesn't mean that she would always be on top of you. She does let us do our own thing but when it really matters she is always there for you, which is great.'

Being the natural competitor he is, Mark's biggest thrill in polo is competing at the top of his chosen sport. 'Playing in the high goal in England is what an English player aims for.' At eighteen he realized his first ambition when putting together a high-goal Beaufort team with brother Luke.

Mark has set his goals much higher since then though, and one he can already tick off the list is winning the Cowdray Gold Cup. 'I never imagined that we would go all the way in 2003, especially as the Hildon Sport team was put together at the last minute. The first time I thought it was possible was when we won in the quarter-finals.' It was an achievement because, as Mark remembers, they were 'killed' by Labegorce by eight goals in the Queen's

Cup. However, all four team members agree that they used the Queen's Cup tournament to get to know each other, iron out mistakes and work out tactics.

When asked what his most important aim is, Mark immediately responds with his unmistakable determination, 'Making it to ten goals because it is the ultimate for a polo player!' He even has the perfect plan set out already. 'If you play and win the Argentine Open you go to ten. So my intention is to keep this vision firmly in my mind.'

But, don't be mistaken, even a young and resolute person like Mark has moments where he has to dig deep, overcome disappointments and keep his career on track. 'It is in the moments I doubt myself that I need to pull myself together and remember that people before me have reached their goal. Even people who might not have been as lucky as Luke and I in benefiting from the background and set-up we have, have succeeded. There are ten-goal players who have just worked very hard and that's what it's all about. Fortunately polo is not a sport where if you haven't done all you needed to do by twenty-one, you have failed. Milo Fernandez-Araujo got to ten in his thirties.'

How does Mark psych himself up and how does he push through the inevitable wall that everybody will encounter at one stage or another? 'For me it's looking back on my successes and imagining further successes by trying to relate them to the present.'

Success must surely be connected to the level of people's self-confidence. Mark tries to remain cool, stable and level-headed and can name the perfect man he would like to emulate for his mental ability. 'The coolest player around is Miguel Novillo-Astrada. You never see his emotions.

'When you lose, you might see it as the end of the world but I try to make myself understand that it is absolutely not the end of the world!'

While playing polo in India, Mark met a player who was 'hot on yoga', and so, for the past couple of years, Mark has been practising yoga and finds it immensely helpful. It involves a lot of stretching which Mark considers hugely important. Not only does it help Mark improve his flexibility, it also helps him mentally. 'I find that I am able to reach balls I was not able to reach before. Also, it involves a lot of breathing exercises to relax both body and mind.' Consequently, Mark does yoga on the mornings of most matches and, when he is not playing, three times a week.

Mark has instinctively always been a forward, attacking player. It is not difficult to see that he invariably gives 150 per cent, putting himself perpetually on the line for his teams, and as Graff Capital, the high-goal team Mark played for in England during 2004 will confirm, 'Having a forward player that gives his all, will boost the entire team's confidence.' Together with brothers Matias and Pablo McDonough, Mark played for patron Markus Graff. In their first season they reached the semi-finals of both the Queen's Cup and the Gold Cup. Mark presumes that he was given the job on the back of his Gold Cup win the year before. 'I was always expecting a call from a team that needed a six

and to have been in a team with Pablo and Matias, two of the best eight-goal players, as well as having a good patron in Markus, has been a lot of fun.'

Although every player always refers to playing polo as 'having fun', I asked Mark whether being a professional polo player is truly always fun? While it is clear that a profession should ideally also be enjoyable and being around horses is very pleasing indeed, Mark admits that of course polo also has its drawbacks. For Mark the biggest drawback is the travelling, which he says is 'great to start with but also very unsettling and stressful', plus, because a profession does not always go well, losing is no fun either! 'If the result goes against you it's definitely

Mark and Luke exchanging views at the end of a chukka during the subsidiary final of the 2003 Warwickshire Cup.

'I am on Grace and Mark is on Otus, an English thoroughbred I bought and gave my Dad and Mark nicked off him!'

Their father, Simon Tomlinson, believes that Mark has a slight advantage over Luke because Mark was much younger when he started playing with really good players.

'Mark has a lot of flair but at the moment he still lacks a bit of discipline on the polo ground. He goes for the ball before the man almost every time and he has to learn that the man is more important.

'Luke has a lot of discipline. He works really hard at his polo. He has worked really hard to get his penalties absolutely right. He is very self-critical yet he can also lift himself very easily. He doesn't get down.'

no fun and can also be quite stressful. The difference that winning and losing makes is incredible. The emotional spectrum is huge; it ranges between being really happy and going out to dinner with your patron and, on the other hand, the patron going off in a huff, perhaps, and you being really disappointed.'

admits to being 'on the edge'. 'You know that there will only be one goal in it and it is in those last minutes of a tight match that you have to try to keep a cool head.' It seems apparent, and Mark underlines this, that it is in those moments players need to draw on all their mental resources. 'The concentration is second to none and, as with any

Mark on Romeo, a homebred gelding during the 2003 Gold Cup final in Deauville.

Mark remembers: 'We had been a bit up against it, playing Marcos Heguy. His team Royal Barrière were about to score and we managed to get the ball. I just got away down the ground about to hit the ball when the mallet broke just as I was making contact with the ball. In this case there is not a lot you can do, it's out of your control really and bad luck!'

When playing against the Beaufort team in the quarter-finals of the 2004 Gold Cup, Mark experienced a close call that could have gone either way. Not only was he playing against his sister Emma, but the match was also level after the sixth chukka and went into overtime. Although playing against a family member does not get to Mark the way it used to, a close call is still a moment when he

profession, the hardest thing to do when you are put under pressure is to tap into your highest level of concentration.'

But one thing is for sure, Mark has all the ingredients of a great polo player and, judging by his talent, determination, attitude and enthusiasm, I am certain that he won't leave a single stone unturned until he reaches his ultimate goal.

It would be wonderful for English polo, as well as for Luke and Mark Tomlinson, if they were to team up not only for Cartier day but also for the Argentine Open and, who knows, they might make history there too!

The Novillo-Astrada Clan

Being one of five gifted, Argentine, polo-playing brothers can, from the outside at least, seem to be quite tricky at times, particularly when each one of them has the same dream: to win the Argentine Open with his brothers.

In December 2003, Eduardo, Miguel, Javier and Ignacio Novillo-Astrada did just that. On this occasion, the youngest out of the quintet, Alejandro, affectionately known as Negro, was left out. This does not, however imply that Negro is in any way less talented or less hungry for success than his siblings. It simply suggests that, because of trailing in age, he has not as yet reached a high enough handicap to be considered for making up the highest possible combined handicap.

Negro, born 15th September 1981, is extremely proud of his brothers' achievements, by the way. 'I am very happy for them and, as long as they are winning, the need to change the team will not arise. I am pleased about that, especially as I still need to improve a lot before I reach their level.'

As the 2004 English high-goal season proved, Alejandro is on the right track. Joining Marcos Heguy and Juan Martin Nero in Stefano Marsaglia's Azzurra team, he made it to the final of the Queen's

Cup and won the Cowdray Gold Cup, a trophy he had, incidentally, already won in 2002 when playing with his brothers Eduardo and Javier for Black Bears at the age of twenty.

All five are extremely close and supportive of each other. When they are not playing as a team in Argentina you will very often find two or even three Astradas playing for the same team. Javier and Eduardo play for Black Bears when in England. In Florida, Miguel and Alejandro play for Gillian Johnston's team Bendabout. Ignacio played the US

The Novillo-Astrada clan! From left to right, starting with the youngest and moving up to the oldest: Alejandro 'Negro', Ignacio 'Nacho', Javier, Miguel and Eduardo.

On seeing this photo Ignacio commented: 'Five of us, that's a lot of polo players! One too many! The sad thing is that only four players make up a team. Soon we will have to sort something out about Alejandro as he is improving a lot!'

Open with Javier and Eduardo for Las Monjitas.

Amazingly, four out of the five brothers have, at one stage in their careers, played for Urs Schwarzenbach's Black Bears. Javier, born 3rd

Javier kept his nose in front of Pablo Spinacci during the opening league match of the 2004 Gold Cup when Black Bears played Labegorce at Anningsley Park, Labegorce's home ground.

On that occasion Black Bears won the match by quite a big margin. Carlos Gracida had to have a substitute step in because he was suffering from food poisoning and, although he started the match, felt too weak to carry on.

December 1975 and the middle brother of the five, was first to meet Urs in 1996. He recalls having played against Urs on numerous occasions when still playing for Ellerston. Some years later a meeting was set up, and Javier, together with Miguel, started to play for Black Bears in 2000.

Because Miguel was also committed to playing with Gillian Johnston, Javier convinced the eldest brother, Eduardo, to join him at Black Bears instead of Miguel.

Eduardo recalls that although he used to work in his father's office and actually loved it, it didn't take much for Javier to persuade him to turn professional and join him. 'My first year as a professional was

2002, and winning the Gold Cup with Black Bears got me off to a good start.' Playing only part-time in Argentina, Eduardo was already playing off nine goals and saw joining Black Bears as a real challenge. 'I wanted to see if I could get a bit better. Also the economic circumstances in Argentina had come to an all-time low so being offered the opportunity to join a top polo team was hard to refuse.' Eduardo remembers having received an offer from another team before but 'It just didn't have the same appeal as playing with Javier and Urs.'

All four who have played for Black Bears agree that not only is it fantastic to be playing for an organization as well structured as Black Bears, but also, more than anything, that Urs is a remarkable person they truly enjoy being with. They are proud to be associated with a patron who will always be part of polo history. Furthermore they enjoy playing with Urs not least because he has a very good understanding of the game.

When Eduardo, Javier and Negro won the 2002 Gold Cup with Urs they used to joke with him and refer to Urs as: 'Our father in England; Urs and us three boys.' And, to this day, Urs himself still refers to them as 'the boys'.

Javier points out that everything at Black Bears works so well, especially behind the scenes, and that playing for such a nice family is just a real pleasure. He also sees his job as: 'An opportunity to keep Black Bears up there winning and making history.' Javier had already won the Gold Cup in 1997 but winning this one with Black Bears meant a lot

because it helped Urs back to holding this fine trophy after an absence of exactly ten years. After winning the Gold Cup in 1992, Black Bears had been very close in 1995 and 2000 but had lost both of these finals; in 2000 Javier and Miguel had been on board.

Miguel too only has good memories of playing for Black Bears. 'Professionally it was a great move because Black Bears have such a good reputation in England. It was similar to getting hired by a formula-one racing team. I always compare polo to a formula-one racing stable because everything has to work smoothly and professionally and with Black Bears it just does!'

No different from his brothers, Miguel also respects and appreciates Urs. 'He is a very fair person and fun to play with. Urs will always tell you exactly what he thinks and, more importantly, his guidelines are always very clear.'

On one point the five brothers are no different from most polo players, in that they are extremely competitive and are in each match to win it! As Javier points out, 'Nobody likes losing and the good thing about polo is that usually when you play well as a team and you make no mistakes, you end up winning.' Ignacio, nicknamed Nacho and the youngest of the Palermo quartet, has of course enjoyed winning yet he also has a very philosophical

Alejandro Novillo-Astrada reaching for the ball just ahead of Mexican Pelon Escapite.

Alejandro was chosen to join Gillian Johnston's team, Bendabout, for the 2004 US Open. Alejandro's team-mates were brother Miguel, Adam Snow and Gillian, but they lost to Catamount in the quarter-final.

'I enjoyed it a lot but I was a bit nervous too, seeing that it was my first twenty-six-goal tournament abroad. Catamount won because they just played better than we did. It really is as simple as that!'

Miguel in a practice chukka
at home on the Novillo-
Astrada farm in Argentina
only days before the final of
the 2003 Argentine Open.

'Playing at home is really
nice. We travel almost all
year round, so being at home
playing with my brothers and
family friends is great. I love
it there. It's really relaxing.
Being there lets us appreciate
the fields we have created.
Having a great set-up at
one's fingertips is a blessing.'

approach to losing. 'I accept defeat. I look at my mistakes and try to improve in time for the next match or tournament. I will just do whatever it takes so as not to repeat the same errors.'

Miguel says it usually takes him two days to get over losing a big match. Yet, at the same time he says that the positive thing he takes away from losing is knowing 'one learns more from losing than from winning'.

When playing in Palermo with his brothers, Nacho admits to probably being the most nervous of the four, which is understandable because 2003 was the first time Nacho played the Argentine Open. 'I was actually nervous the whole season, from the moment my

brothers told me that I was going to play with them! Eduardo, Miguel and Javier had always done so well in the Open. They were never out of the top four, and so I was afraid that with me on the team they might end up outside the top four.'

When I pointed out that his fears were not really justified as he clearly must have been the needed missing link because, prior to him joining them, the three brothers had never done better than reaching the top four, Nacho produced a modest smile. When asked what he thought he had brought to the team he explained that, by playing with them he made them bring out the best in each other. 'I always told my brothers that they would have to make an extra effort because they would have to carry me a bit. Their understanding of this effectively brought out the very best in all of us.'

Winning the open on his first attempt did also slightly change Nacho's life. 'I now have to try to

Alejandro, 'Negro', in a match against Broncos during the 2004 Queen's Cup tournament.

Marcos Heguy spotted Alejandro's talent when he saw him playing in the United States, and Negro responded thus. 'I'd like to think that Marcos invited me to play with him for Azzurra because he thought I played well! Polo is a very small community where everybody knows everbody. So if you happen to be playing well, the word spreads quickly!'

Marcos was proved to be right as he got a five-goal player who was playing more like a six-goaler. In fact Negro was put up to six after Azzurra won the 2004 Gold Cup. 'The biggest ambition I want to achieve is to become a ten-goal player. It is possible if you work hard and believe strongly enough that you can do it.'

stay up there at the top which is the most difficult thing to do.' Nacho feels that he has to take his polo even more seriously and work ever harder at it. Above all he wants to improve. In Nacho's mind one thing is clear: he wants to prove to everybody that the brothers' win has not been a one-off. He believes that the four are under much more pressure now!

The decision for the Novillo-Astradas to finally form a team together came about because Gonzalito Pieres, with whom they had played for the previous two years, wanted to play with his cousins. Javier explains: 'When we first sat down with Gonzalito we agreed to play together for two years with the intention of revising the situation, always bearing in mind that Nacho would eventually join us.'

Nacho, born 21st March 1978, wanted to finish his business studies before turning professional at the age of twenty-one. Although he has no regrets about having put his studies ahead of polo for the time it took him to get his degree, he is now fully ready to take the polo world by storm. 'I made the choice to turn professional mostly because I wanted to play the Argentine Open and nowadays you have to be a professional player if you want to succeed and dedicate your life to it.'

So, although Nacho did not have the time to improve his handicap and was lacking in experience as well as horsepower, the decision was taken. The four brothers were going to try to get a step closer to realizing their dream. Eduardo, Miguel and Javier all chipped in and provided Nacho with most of his horses for the Argentine season.

The decision was taken in April 2003, and Javier remembers making his grandfather a very happy man when telling him that the four of them were going to play together, naming their team after his farm, La Aguada! 'My grandfather had just turned ninety when I told him and he was just over the moon! This, in turn, pumped us up even more. We were conscious of making Nacho welcome. We wanted to put him at ease and, reflecting on it, playing as a family really did bring out the best in us.'

Everyone could see that the four truly gave meaning to the saying 'blood is thicker than water'. And, as Adolfo Cambiaso, who played the final the importance of improving their communication skills within the team. She pointed out that being brothers added another dimension to the challenge as it is probably tougher to accept criticism or advice from a sibling. Seeing the psychologist once a week created a safe environment for the brothers to

against them, put it: 'The four brothers boosted each other up. I believe that if you play with someone you really want to play with, it automatically makes you gain a goal in handicap.'

Even though this may be true, the four brothers also decided to seek help from sports psychologist Nelly Gisgaffre for the duration of the Argentine polo season. All four agree that the main benefit they gained from seeing the psychologist was to see talk openly about what was on their minds.

Javier believes that although resolving a situation can sometimes be harder between brothers it is also better because 'you can never get really irrevocably angry with your brothers'.

'Seeing the psychologist united us more than we already were. It improved our team spirit and on the field this translated into a total understanding. It was almost on a different level than we had experienced

Miguel playing for Gillian Johnston's team, Graffham, in the quarter-final of the 2003 Veuve Cliquot Gold Cup.

When playing in England, Gillian keeps all the team's horses on her farm in Graffham, a village only a stone's throw away from Cowdray.

'I have known Gillian forever. Our fathers used to play polo together in the US.'

Eduardo and Miguel playing practice chukkas at home. Eduardo is on Puma his 'absolute best horse'.

'I feel great playing at home. We have a lot of fun playing practice chukkas. When we are back in Argentina the five of us spend a lot of time together. When we were younger we often couldn't finish the practice chukkas because we got so angry with each other that we started fighting. My father had to step in and ended up sending us to have a shower to cool down!'

before.' As if by magic, they were all on the same wavelength and, as Javier remembers, 'We hardly had to talk during chukkas.'

All four are also united in appreciating how much the experience had helped them mentally. Most of the matches, especially the semi-finals, had all been very close matches and the boys agree that the mental strength they had acquired helped their self-belief enormously. No matter how united they seem as a team, however, they are still very different in character.

Eduardo, born 7th October 1972, describes himself as a hyperactive person who can never stay in one place for too long. 'I like to be moving all the time. Whether it is going to the farm, to the beach or doing any other sport. I also enjoy a bit of nightlife with my friends, whereas my brothers are quite happy staying at home.' Eduardo also loves being a father to his twin boys. 'They are my best friends actually and I do everything with them.' Eduardo's wife Tina has to remind him at times that he is their father and not their brother, particularly when they need a bit of a firmer, educating hand.

What Eduardo likes best about polo is being outdoors, around horses and in touch with nature. He also enjoys the great variety of people and cultures the game allows him to mix with. 'I love the fact that you have the grooms, some of whom have never been to school, as well as the top businessmen of the world all drinking *mate* together and sitting around an *asado*. This is only possible in polo and the funny thing is that from the outside you would never think this possible! The bottom line is that I love horses; we all do, which is probably the reason for the uniting of different backgrounds and cultures, and for the social barriers to get sidelined.'

Eduardo is also probably the most religious one of the brothers. Before a match one can often see him hands together quietly gathering his thoughts. He admits that before the Open in Palermo he made some promises and that before every match he went to a big cathedral to pray. Reflecting on it, Eduardo jokingly concludes that it seemed to have worked out quite well and that he thinks he ought to keep on doing it!

Miguel, the second one in line, was born on 10th February 1974 and is probably the quietest and most level-headed one out of the five. He always seems very together and speaking with him confirmed that he is also very focused. After the win in Palermo, it 'was like a dream come true' to be rewarded with the highest handicap. 'Becoming a ten-goal player was one of my objectives ever since I was very young! However, now that I have reached it I feel like I am having to work even harder to keep it.' Miguel explains that it is as difficult to become a ten-goal player as it is to stay one. It is also quite a different matter. 'To become a ten-goal player takes a

Javier during the 2002 Veuve Cliquot Gold Cup final.

'That match was really tough. Fortunately Negro scored our winning goal in the last seconds of the match!'

In the USA Javier is playing off a ten-goal handicap, but in Europe and Argentina he is still rated a nine. 'It would be really great to be rated a ten-goal player around the world and, in a way, I was hoping to have my handicap raised to ten in Argentina after the incredible season I had in 2003. But, at the end of the day, winning is more important to me; it proves more.'

lot of time and hard work. Once you are there it becomes a mental thing. You are conscious of what you have achieved and now you have to work hard at maintaining your standard.'

Miguel became a professional polo player at nineteen and it took him ten years to reach his ten-goal ambition. In England he is, however, still rated a nine-goal player which he puts down to not having won one of the major English tournaments. Sadly his 2004 season in England never really took off because Miguel sustained an injury before the Queen's Cup tournament had even started. Brother Nacho was flown in to take Miguel's spot with Geebung.

Ignacio, 'Nacho', playing for Geebung in the quarter-final of the 2004 Gold Cup hitting an under-the-neck shot. Nacho came over to England earlier than expected as he had to replace brother Miguel who got injured before the beginning of the Queen's Cup.

'I was coming anyway to play in the Gold Cup because Miguel had other commitments playing in the US. This is my first season playing in England. I had a lot of fun playing for Geebung. The standard of polo was great and Geebung had very good and competitive horses. This horse played a great tournament. I scored a half-field goal on her!'

Nacho and Alejandro played against each other in the quarter-final of the 2004 Gold Cup.

'Alejandro is having a great season. He was near the goal, hitting for goal, and I went for a bump trying to avoid getting hit by his mallet. I knew I had to cover myself because Negro was going for a big hit! I managed to put him off enough for him not to score!'

Analysing the success of Palermo, Miguel thinks that it came down to truly playing as a team. 'We got along so well and were even able to switch horses around amongst us without creating any problems. This meant that we got the best out of all our horses because some horses do go better for another player even if it doesn't belong to him. We were able to recognize that and acted upon it.'

Miguel points out that organizing the right horses between them made a huge difference. Trailing by three goals coming into the last two chukkas of the Open, he believes that their horses were better than those of La Dolfina. 'Ours were more ready and ran better. Also, from the first chukka to the very last we stuck to our plan, which was playing man to man with the view of trying to open up the game. We didn't mind who we played as long as we kept to our plan. Of course when you play against Adolfo Cambiaso, part of the plan will inevitably also be to stop him from getting the ball.'

Miguel is very clear about why he is a polo player and simply says that it is because he followed his dream. If he had not done so, he thinks that he might have gone into private banking, managing portfolios.

On the polo field, Miguel sees his strength in trying hard to make the best use of his team-mates. On an emotional level, polo represents a vehicle enabling him to achieve his objectives. Miguel is passionate about polo yet concedes that he can get tired of competing all the time. 'Stopping for a week can be good because it makes me eager to play again!'

Miguel also claims that jumping from one horse to another during a match does not mean that he is not fully aware of which horse he is on and what he can demand from any particular horse. In fact, he goes as far as saying that he would recognize the horse he was riding even if he was blindfolded!

Religion is important to the Novillo-Astrada family. The main things in Miguel's life are, God, his family and then polo. Miguel believes that God runs the world and that God wants him to be a good example for polo!

All the brothers remember being introduced to polo by their father and, in particular, by their grandfather who was 'crazy about polo'. They

remember going to see the Argentine Open as young boys knowing that one day they would be champions too. They saw the Heguys play with their father and dreamt of winning the Argentine Open on its 100th anniversary. In the end it took them a little longer because their father was not a professional polo player and did not leave the boys a ready-made set-up from which to start. As a family, however, the Novillo-Astradas pulled together and worked really hard at creating a good set-up.

It might have taken them ten years longer than planned, but winning not only the Argentine Open but also the Triple Crown (the three major tournaments of the Argentine season) on the 110th anniversary is surely one-up on their original dream. And, having 'La Aguada' engraved on the trophy for that anniversary made it an even more memorable event.

Ignacio, Miguel, Eduardo and Javier played together for the first time in the Argentine Open, 2003. As La Aguada, they not only won the Open (Abierto) itself but also the Abierto de Tortugas and the Abierto de Hurlingham, which meant that they made history by winning the Triple Crown: the three major tournaments of the Argentine polo season. Not only did each and every one of the four brothers fulfil a lifetime's ambition but they certainly also achieved a very special dream, winning *en famille*!

POLO IN ACTION

(Opposite and left) Matt Lodder and Jesus Eloy 'Pelon' Escapite in the all-decisive league match between England and Mexico, F.I.P. World Championships, Chantilly 2004.

Owing to very heavy rain, the match between England and Mexico had to be stopped in midflow after the second chukka. The remainder of the match was then rescheduled from the Saturday to the following Wednesday. Meanwhile both teams had both won and lost a match in their group. This meant that the winner of their encounter was granted entry into the semi-final.

Pelon Escapite, captain of the Mexican team, recalls the match.

'The match against England was a tough experience because the president decided to change our team for it. Yet we, the players, felt that it was not necessary. This meant that we were not concentrating as much as we should have been. The fact that the play was interrupted owing to heavy rain and that we had to finish the match some days later actually helped us because we got killed out there at the beginning of the match! After beating Brazil we gained confidence, and so we played much better in the second half of the England match. England only scored four goals in four chukkas as opposed to scoring seven goals in two chukkas! Still, England beat us which meant that they made it into the semi-finals.'

Pelon, a four-goal player, fell in love with the game of polo at the age of ten.

'I look up to Carlos Gracida. Right from the start I had it in mind to become a professional player one day.

'When you are playing for your country, as here in Chantilly, you are expected to give everything and you don't only do it for yourself. You do it out of pride and for all the fans who have travelled so far to support you. You play for your flag!'

Australian Jack 'Rookie' Baillieu just about to score in the tightly contested league match for the J.D. Macleod Cup against Elysian Fields, Ellerston 2004. Close at Rookie's heels is Mike Todd.

Rookie was given his nickname when he first started playing polo competitively. 'I was the new kid on the block. My parents called me Rookie and soon it was the name everybody knew me by; it stuck, I had no choice!'

'Here I'm running towards goal with Mike Todd hot on my tail trying to hook me. In polo you have to have good vision so that you are absolutely aware of having someone behind you trying to hook you. Here I was fortunately far enough ahead for him not to catch me. I'm on Pearl, a horse my patron, Ronnie, lent me.'

Mike Todd started playing polo at fourteen and has been with Michael King and Elysian Fields for the past three years. Mike started to coach patron Michael King when the two first met and has been helping him ever since. According to Michael: 'He does everything, including running the polo side of my farm in Queensland.'

Mike says: 'My challenge is to put Elysian Fields on the map, worldwide. The farm is beautiful and the facilities there are great. It's thirty-five minutes from the Gold Coast in Queensland. Also I want to see Michael get better and Elysian do well. Simultaneously I am also trying to find an additional career because a career in polo doesn't last forever, and so I am also learning about business and property with Michael.'

Mike has been going to Ellerston since it held its first tournaments, fourteen years ago, and comments on the J.D. Macleod Cup in 2004.

'The game was very fast and furious, my job was to mark Rookie and take him out of the game. I was trying to hook him all day! We won by one goal. Ellerston is a fantastic place. They have the best facilities in the world with fabulous grounds. I call it polo wonderland; it is beautifully landscaped and the Packers are amazing to everybody.'

Mike has won a fair amount of tournaments in his career including the Melbourne Cup in 1987 and Ellerston in 2000. However, as Mike puts it, 'Winning in life is winning the biggest tournament!'

Rookie Baillieu, Wastecorp, in pursuit of the ball during the 2004 J.D. Macleod Cup semi-final at Ellerston. His shadow is Rob Archibald who played for the Garangula team.

Wastecorp won the semis yet lost to Gonzalito Pieres, Matias MacDonough, Johnny Williams and Andrew Blake Thomas, the Ellerston team, in the final.

'We played terribly in the final! Our horses were dead! I played five horses during the entire tournament and they were really tired by the end of the month. I have been in a final at Ellerston before and won by over ten goals. It's just that sometimes it goes your way and sometimes it doesn't. Sure, you feel disappointed. I used to take losing very hard when I was younger. But you have to experience the good with the bad. I learned to look at it more objectively and to understand the reasons why you lose. Sometimes they are reasons you cannot control. In this case it was the horsepower.'

Gerardo 'Toto' Collardin, Talandracas, and Rookie Baillieu, Geebung, in the 2004 Veuve Cliquot Gold Cup tournament, Cowdray.

Gerardo was given his nickname by his parents.

'The name 'Toto' came from a children's television programme! I really like being called Toto. It's much shorter than Gerardo!'

Like most Argentine players, Toto started playing polo at a very early age on his father's farm. Later he also joined the Indios Polo Club, home to all the Heguys, and in 1995 Toto turned professional. Although 2004 was only the second time Talandracas had played in England, Toto had been with patron Edouard Carmignac for four years, and together they won the 2001 Gold Cup in Sotogrande. With Santa Maria, Toto won the Silver Cup twice. One of his bigger triumphs was winning the Copa Cámara de Diputados in 1998, the same year he won the World Championships for Argentina in Santa Barbara.

Rookie too had always been interested in horses, and had grown up with them on his parents' farms. Rookie was introduced to polo by his father who played as an amateur. Having gone to boarding school, Rookie never really got a chance to play much until after he left school at eighteen.

'I picked it up very quickly because I could ride, and here I am a professional! For me, polo has everything: it allows you to travel the world and to meet some amazing people, and it is a sport that has a lot more components than any other sport. The fact that you play on horseback and that every horse moves and reacts differently makes polo pretty special. You have to master the horsemanship as well as playing the game. It's a sport where no one can reach perfection. We all just aspire to be as good as we can and to get the best horses we can.'

Gerardo 'Toto' Collardin, Talandracas, on the ball in a tight battle with Horacio Etcheverry, Grassfield, at the 2003 Deauville Gold Cup.

This had been Toto's second year playing in Deauville.

'I'm on Marcelo, a horse my father bred. I always travel with my horses whether it's to England or to France. Here I'm just concentrating on the ball. At the same time I'm trying to be aware of who might be coming up from behind in case it is one of my team-mates because you might leave the ball for him, to give him a clear run. Horacio is a nice guy and a great player. The disappointing thing in Deauville was the field. It was such a disaster! Hitting the ball was really not easy. I got a bit upset especially as, inevitably, all you could think about was that you wanted to play on a better field.'

Rookie Baillieu and Henry Brett at Cartier International Day, Guards 2002.

The Rest of the Commonwealth team comprising Rookie, Glen Gilmore, Simon Keyte and Fred Mannix, took on and beat England. 'Winning the Coronation Cup was amazing! It is the biggest cup I have ever won!'

Henry Brett of the England team remembers it being a really tight game.

'They scored the winning goal when I met the ball, hitting it on the nearside right in front of the goal; the ball hit Simon Keyte's horse's knee and went into the goal! It was just an unlucky hit. Instead of the ball going through and us escaping, it bounced back and into the goal!'

Henry has been a professional polo player since the age of seventeen.

'It was always going to be polo because I left school at the age of fifteen, without GCSEs, and started working in stables. I had a dream: to be the best I could be. I always knew I was good and believed in myself, which some people might interpret as

being a bit arrogant but I feel that one has to have self-belief if one is to succeed in life. It also depends on how you come across. I am very happy to be where I'm at because I don't come from a horse-minded family. Both my parents knew nothing about horses. I got my first pony when my parents sold a sofa, and we kept the pony in our garage in Oxford. This is how I started riding.

'I am most certainly an outsider who has come into the game. I was mad about polo from the word go. I used to always be quite quick on the field. I am not the most physical player and I'm OK with the ball, but I think that I'm now developing as a polo player. I am beginning to read the game better and to know when to play which shots in which situation. Tactics come into polo a lot and if you watch any good player, it would be this understanding that sets them apart from the rest. It is not because they might be better with the ball.'

Argentine Pancho Bensadon, Isla Carroll, at
the 2004 US Open final.

Pancho and the other team members,
Memo Gracida, Sugar Erskine and patron
John Goodman, beat White Birch ten goals to
six. Pancho was definitely the man to watch
as he scored an impressive eight goals in the
match. In fact Pancho had already been very
much in form leading up to the final by
providing most of his team's goals.

Team-mate and Mexican all-time great
Memo Gracida praised Pancho saying that he
had had a fantastic tournament. 'He played
well above his handicap!'

Pancho, a full cousin to all the Heguys
who are currently playing, has been
concentrating on getting well mounted and
organized in the USA for the past eight
years. Now that he has succeeded, he would
love to come and play in Europe too.
Winning the 2004 US Open meant a lot to
Pancho.

'Winning was a great feeling, notably
because I was playing with Memo Gracida. To
be playing with a player of that level is very
special. Also, it was the first time we had
actually played together in a tournament.
We had played some exhibition matches and
practice chukkas together but never a
tournament. Memo is very organized, and
when playing with him you can feel the
power of a great organization.

'As a team we had a lot of confidence
before the tournament. One can say that on
paper we were actually favourites. We
didn't, however, get off to a very good start
and nobody thought that we could be
champions, but we managed to get our
rhythm and the horses improved, which, in
turn, helped us gain the confidence we
needed. The fact that people had put us
down helped us and brought out the best in
us. We drew strength from it and managed
to prove them wrong. Yes it's true, I scored
many goals but it was still down to great
teamwork! My job? Well, one of my jobs was
to score and so I am happy that I did.'

Guy Schwarzenbach, Garangula, and Bernard Roux, patron of Hyde Hill, during the 14–16-goal Garangula tournament, November 2003.

A further two teams, Elysians Fields and Ellerston, took part in the tournament. The Garangula team, with Schwarzenbach father and son, and cousins Simon Keyte and John Paul Clarkin, won all their league matches including this semi-final match against Hyde Hill and the final itself.

Guy's passion for polo has not only been fueled by his father's love for the sport but, having gone to school at Eton, he was also encouraged to play polo there. Guy won the National School Championship for Eton in 2000.

'Garangula was the first tournament I played at that level. It was a huge experience. JP and Simon play so well together. It is extraordinary to play with them. My father and I just had to position ourselves well! I definitely

learned a lot playing the tournament. Also, it was so much faster than the polo I had been accustomed to; I quickly learned that one has to be at the right place at the right time!'

Other than polo, Guy loves climbing. In the summer of 2004 he teamed up with some friends from school and did the three-peak challenge. 'You have to climb Snowdon in Wales, Scafell Pike in the Lake District and Ben Nevis in Scotland all in twenty-four hours. It's a common challenge and a lot of people do it in the summer. I love nature combined with a challenge and climbing gives you that. It is fantastic! It's all about teamwork; you need to develop a real trust in each other. What I also love about it is that you get the feeling of being totally away from everything. It's magical!'

Bernard has been coming to Garangula for the past four years. He lives in Melbourne and keeps most of the Hyde Hill horses with Damien Johnston in Queensland where the weather is just much nicer all year round.

'I keep one or two in Melbourne in order to keep fit. I started playing polo in 1985 on the east coast of America in New Jersey. I came back to Australia in 1986 and met Damien, who was only seventeen at the time, and I sent him to Adam Snow. In 1988, Adam, Damien, Mike Todd and I won the Melbourne Cup playing Ellerston. Our team was called Mount Dunmore, but our nickname was "the Kids Team" because we were all so young at the time! Polo is in my blood, and once it's in the blood, it stays forever! Polo is definitely a passion and it also keeps me young! Whether you are winning or losing, the important thing is playing. My ambition is to play high goal in England with Adam and Damien.

'Playing against Guy was fun. He is an extraordinary athlete and a very talented young man. You could feel his desire to win. Garangula is simply an idyllic place, a real mecca for polo and the Schwarzenbachs are lovely hosts.'

John Paul Clarkin and Urs Schwarzenbach both played for Garangula at Garangula's November 2003 tournament. Both are heading in pursuit of play but Urs seems to be sitting on the faster horse!

'Horsepower is very important because no matter how great a player is, if he is too slow getting to where he should be, the other player is always going to beat him!'

On his farm in Garangula Urs also breeds horses.

'The important point is that, as a patron or professional polo player you are trying to get the best horses you can. Everybody does! You have to get the horses however you can. You can buy them, you can steal them and you can breed them; I really don't care as long as I have the best! Our breeding programme at Garangula is not very scientific. At present I don't do embryo transplants like they do in Argentina. We do it the old-fashioned way. I'd rather let nature take it's course but, recently, we have put some semen aside from a stallion of ours that has a great track record, but he is coming to the end of his shelf life. Breeding is great, but I don't have the ambition to win the Gold Cup on a homebred string, but it would, of course, be different if one was to breed the Derby or the Grand National winner. Sure, it is nice to get the odd champion which is homebred, otherwise you would be questioning why you go through it all. Breeding is fun but it is not the be-all and end-all.'

Marek Dochnal, patron of Larchmont, and Urs Schwarzenbach, patron of Black Bears, both play at number one in their teams. Maybe new kid on the block Marek is watching longtimer Urs's move closely, hoping for a tip or two, because 2004 was, after all, Marek's first ever high-goal polo season.

Urs, on the other hand, started his first high-goal polo season back in 1988! Then again, seeing that Larchmont beat Black Bears in the 2004 Queen's Cup quarter-final, Urs might just be remembering how he felt in his first high-goal season.

'I like Marek, he seems a good guy! How long he will be able to stay in the sport will depend on how he can cope with the pressure.'

Marek speaks about his hopes for the future.

'I am sure that we will win the Queen's Cup or the Gold Cup in the near future. It will be the consequence of our dedication to polo. It might not be very modest of me to say, but I believe that in a couple of years we will win all the big tournaments! We will have the best horses and the best players. It's funny because we hadn't planned to enter the high-goal tournament in 2004. We were concentrating on improving my polo but then Piki told me that I would get bored staying at the farm so he suggested we enter the high-goal tournaments. So, one could say that I was thrown in the deep end! I was pretty stressed and nervous for my first high-goal match but it got better throughout the season.'

(Opposite and left) New Zealander John Paul Clarkin playing for Garangula at the J.D. Macleod Cup at Ellerston, March 2004.

'The grounds at Ellerston are just phenomenal. There are simply no better ones in the entire world! The whole infrastructure is second to none. To be playing there is a great privilege. The polo is also different in Ellerston because of the sheer speed which results from the quality of the fields. Very few players miss the ball which makes the game so much faster. There are hardly any divots which means the ball very seldom bounces away from you and, because of this, you also have to be a bit sharper and anticipate the play more. You can't afford to gamble for a miss because if you do that you might as well wait at the halfway because the opponent will have scored a goal!

'The backhander is a shot you have to be able to do in your sleep and, fortunately, it is a shot that comes naturally to me. I think one thing that people seem to get wrong is believing that, because it is a backhander they have to hit it from further back, which I don't believe to be right. I think that you have to hit it more or less in the same spot as a forehand which gives you more leverage to hit the ball. When playing at number four, as I often do, there is nothing better than hitting a good backhand and seeing your team run off in the other direction with the ball.

'As for the neck shot, it's an impressive shot when it comes off, but you have to be careful not to whack yourself on the head with a whoopee stick! It is a shot that can be used both for attack and defence. Also, if you connect well with this shot you do get the right feeling.'

JP Clarkin, Garangula, and Mike King, patron of Elysian Fields, during the 2003 Garangula semi-final.

Mike King named his polo team and farm in Queensland, Elysian Fields. 'It means a state or place of perfect bliss, which to me is the rolling green hills of my farm.' Mike has been playing polo for six years. 'I saw a game and fell in love with it! As for Garangula, I love that place. It's one of the prettiest places in Australia, or even in the world. The fields are magnificent. You always have a fantastic time there. I'm sure to be going back there as long as I get invited. I played the final in 2002 and was beaten by Ellerston.

This tournament was the first time Simon Keyte and JP played together in Australia. JP was thrilled to get the call.

'Garangula had been through a few players, they needed a new combination and I was lucky to be in line for the job.

'Playing with Mr. S. and Guy was a lot of fun. They both played well. This photo is from the semis, but the mare I am riding on the attack is the one I got Champion Pony for in the final. She is a New Zealand Thoroughbred called "Y". She was sixteen there – and was actually in foal at the time – and has since been retired. "Y" gave you everything you ever wanted from a horse. In my opinion she made all the difference, especially in the final! She belongs to Mr. S. and had played over in England for Black Bears for quite a few years. This year she was sent over to Australia to retire.

'The other horse belongs to Rick McCarthy. We pulled in a few reinforcements and leased some additional horses from Rick; this one was a very good horse.'

JP Clarkin and Matt Lodder keeping an eye on the play during the 2003 Veuve Cliquot Gold Cup; Hildon Sport won the match by beating Dubai.

JP's fifth season in England was in 2003, and he has always been based in or around Cirencester.

'I have been playing for the Vesteys for years and am lucky enough to have my base with them. It is fantastic because they have a great set-up with all the facilities one needs. I started playing twelve goal with the Vesteys and, since then, we have moved on through to high goal together.

'The semi against Dubai was the bigger hurdle on paper than the final against Labegorce. Going into the match we felt like we had absolutely nothing to lose. Going into the last chukkas 4–3 behind it was a matter of do or die and throwing everything at it! We were fortunate enough to get up by one goal. Then Dubai clawed back and we just managed to scrape the last one in. All this gave us great confidence coming into the final because, after all, we had just beaten the favourites!

'The reason we won the semi was sheer determination! Mark and Luke were desperately marking Lolo and Adolfo. Nina was just running, stretching out; and I did what I had to do and got stuck with Matt Lodder a lot of the time! We just thought of spreading out more and that's what we did in the last chukka. Dubai just couldn't stop us.'

Ben Vestey, Foxcote, and Guy Schwarzenbach, Black Bears, playing a league match for the 2004 Warwickshire Cup, at Ashton Down, Cirencester.

For Ben this was the first high-goal game of the season and for Guy it was his first high-goal game!

Ben started playing polo with the Cotswold Hunt Pony Club at the age of eight. He is the middle child, sandwiched between his two sisters, Tamara and Nina. The children had been playing polo together right from the start. Now that Ben has joined the Household Cavalry he plays polo a little less than he used to. The Foxcote team, with Ben and Tamara Vestey, won the Warwickshire Cup in 2002.

'Until then there had been a thirty-year gap since a Foxcote team had won anything. In this 2004 match, playing with Nina, we started off incredibly slowly and Black Bears got off to a 7–2 lead. But really, I felt that we were getting back into the game during the fifth chukka. We got within two goals and then they stretched off again! Playing against such horsepower is so difficult! Every chukka, Black Bears come out on horses as good as the ones in the chukka before! Here I'm on Abuela, an eight-year-old mare, just over from Argentina. It was her first season and, when a horse comes over, it normally takes a year to settle in but Abuela has come in straight away and is one of my best horses. I played her in the fifth chukka which is one of the most important chukkas. She has been fantastic all season. She is a very natural horse, she does everything; you don't even have to ask her and she does it all for you!'

At this Warwickshire Cup match, Guy replaced his father Urs at number one. A few months before, Guy had had his first taste of good polo when he teamed up with his father, Simon Keyte and JP Clarkin for the Garangula tournament.

'My first high-goal match with Black Bears was a great experience! It was even faster and better than the polo I played in Garangula! It's a real reason for me to continue playing at that level! It has evoked a real ambition to keep playing. I have only just started my own business, and if the means are there I will most certainly form a team one day. Give me a couple of years and I will be there.

'Playing against Ben was fun. He is very nice and a good player, and is my brother-in-law's cousin. Unfortunately I don't see too much of him.'

JP Clarkin, Garangula, and James Beim, Ellerston, at the 2003
Garangula final. JP is on the grey mare called Camouflage, a New
Zealand mare Garangula bought for their breeding programme.

'I'm travelling at full blast towards goal. No doubt Simon is in
front of me, that's why you can see me yelling quite loud! It also
looks like I'm about to keep "Beimie" out of the way!

'The final was a tough match but I think we played well as a
team that day; Guy played well and everyone pulled together. In
fact, we didn't lose one match during the entire tournament.
Once you are in a final though it's anyone's game. Luckily that
day it was ours!

'Personally, I don't tend to get too nervous playing in a final. I
probably get a bit more tense depending on who I am playing
against and whether it's in front of a huge crowd or not.'

(Above and opposite) New Zealander Tommy Wilson played the 2004 eighteen-goal J.D. Macleod Cup tournament at Ellerston for Millamolong Gold. In the quarter-final match, Millamolong Gold was drawn against the eventual Cup winners, Ellerston.

Tommy started his professional career as a two-goal player some thirteen years ago. At the time of the tournament, Tommy played off a seven-goal handicap.

'To progress in the tournament we had to win this match, yet we lost by two goals. In both photos I'm on Mace, a horse provided by James Ashton, patron of the team. In fact all the horses I rode were provided by James. He mounted me very well and made the team very competitive.'

In the photo above, Tommy is being marked by English player Andrew Blake Thomas.

'I'm trying to run around the outside of Andrew with the ball in control, using the speed of the horse to get ahead of him as he is trying to ride me off. Mace's ears are perked up. She seems ready and knows what is expected from her. Actually it looks like she is looking at goal, while I'm trying to hit the ball, as if to tell me where I should be aiming for!'

In the other photo, Gonzalito Pieres is trying to disrupt Tommy's action.

'I am at full speed and, by the looks of it, Gonzalito is putting me under immense pressure on a very good Ellerston horse! I am just trying to take control of the ball and the horse at the same time, which is very difficult, particularly if the ball is bouncing and you are travelling at full speed!

'When I think of polo I feel the enjoyment I get from something I am very passionate about. I would have loved to have played rugby professionally but I am very satisfied with the decision I have made. Playing polo enables me to get around the world, and I feel very honoured to be asked to play for various teams.'

Argentine player Bartolome 'Lolo' Castagnola connecting well with the ball in a league match for the 2003 Queens Cup. Dubai played the Black Cats on their home ground in Holyport.

'This forehand strike went far! It is a great swing! I connected well with the ball and it is flying as straight as an arrow. I would guess that the ball travelled 100 yards. Perfect!'

South African Sugar Erskine during the 100th US Open, which took place in Wellington, Florida, in April 2004.

The red shirts of Isla Carroll beat Peter Brant's White Birch by 10–6. It was the second time that the two teams had met in the US Open final. Isla Carroll came up with the goods on both occasions.

In 2004 Sugar played a big part in that victory. After the match Memo Gracida was full of praise for him. 'Sugar, is a warrior. He never gives up. He works really hard. He played very well defensively. Usually we have him attacking, but in the final he played more in defence.'

For Sugar himself, winning felt like a dream.

'I felt honoured just to have had the Isla Carroll jersey on! I also felt honoured to have been on a team with Memo Gracida. I was only two years old when Memo won his first US Open in 1977. Ten years ago, I was just starting out, messing around. I feel very grateful to John Goodman for having taken me under his wing. Now the win has sort of sunk in but at first I had to keep pinching myself. Winning the 2004 Open was unexpected. Something was helping us along the way to reach the final, and by the time we got to the final we were really pumped up. We wanted to play the final even two days before we got there! Winning it with John was fabulous. It was really cool because it was the second time for each of us and to be doing it together felt great.'

Sugar first won the US Open in 1998 with brothers Sebastian and Pite Merlos and Nicolas Roldan, when the team beat John Goodman for whom Sugar was playing in 2004.

Pepe Araya and Sugar Erskine in the 2003 final of the Copa Cámara de Diputados, Palermo.

The Cámara is a very big tournament in the Argentine polo calendar. It runs parallel to the Open itself. Teams that do not qualify for the Argentine Open can enter the qualifying stages for the Cámara de Diputados. In 2003 Pepe Araya and his three brothers didn't qualify for the Open but, as Coronel Suárez, they won the qualifier for the Cámara and reached the final of the tournament itself.

'The Cámara is very competitive. In 2003 six teams entered, the same number as for the Open. To give you an idea of the standard of play, the handicap went up to thirty.

'Sadly we lost but it was a real pleasure to be playing with my three brothers and to have reached the final. We did have our chances and we were very close, but this is polo. The good thing about polo is that, at some point, you will have the opportunity for a rematch, and so all you need to do is to keep trying, keep on improving and the fortunes will turn. The main thing is to always come off the field knowing that you have tried your best and, in the case of a defeat, you have to tell yourself "bad luck" and admit that the other team was better.

'Here I am playing Tango, a stallion we bred and whose mother won Best Playing Pony in 1983 when my father and Benjamin won the Argentine Open. We still breed with Tango. He plays the Argentine season from September to December and then attends to his breeding duties. If you were to ask him what he prefers I am sure he would say breeding!

'Sugar is a great player and a friend. He stood-in for me during the World Cup one year when I got injured, and he played my horses.'

During the English high-goal season, Pepe Araya usually stays with the Tomlinsons, playing with them and other people.

'We have become close friends over the years. I enjoy it a lot there. My father played with Claire and Simon before me, back in 1981. They have always remained friends and so it was easy for me to continue our relationship.'

In 2003 Pepe played for Ladyswood. They entered the Warwickshire Cup and, in this match, were drawn against Foxcote Red.

'I'm on Ivana in a bit of a ride-off fight with Nina Vestey. It looks like I am beating her on that occasion. My mare Ivana likes winning ride-offs, particularly when I am on the right side. She puts everything into it! Nina is such a good player that you cannot afford to take much notice of the fact that she is a lady because she can score as many goals as she wants; and so right from the start I have to put that at the back of my mind! In the first picture you can see that my mare was pushing really hard, and in the second picture we have the proof that she won the battle! Horses know what is expected from them when they are in that situation. I have been playing Ivana for some time and, believe me, she knows what to do and enjoys it! Some horses, when put in that situation, even make an extra effort to keep winning the ride-offs.'

Taking the horses out for an early morning swim or gallop on the beach during the Deauville tournament has become a bit of a tradition. Pepe Araya, here on his horse Garua, took his string out one morning and couldn't resist letting rip along the beach!

'Having the chance to take the horses to the beach early in the morning is fabulous. We take them into the water, swim them a bit, then they roll in the sand. They really love it; it's like being wild and free! Garua is a horse we bred but I've sold him now. His dam was ridden by my father when he won the Open in 1983, and so there is a a bit of history in this picture.

'Being on the beach helps the horses to relax. Deauville is in August, towards the end of the season, and the horses are all a bit tired and bored with being stuck in the stables. Going to the beach is a welcome change for them, and I must say that I enjoy it a lot too! After Deauville I usually go back to England for ten days before heading back to Argentina.'

Pepe Araya played for Ladyswood
during the 2003 Deauville Gold Cup.
In this match against Royal Barrière,
Pepe is about to turn the play
around.

'It looks like I am about to hit an
open back-hander. It's one of my
favourite shots; a shot, when you get
the time to hit it, that is quite an
easy one and you can really throw
your whole body into it. You can hit
it quite a distance. The secret is to
keep your eye on the ball and to
really hit it by putting all the weight
of your body through the mallet.'

Lucas Monteverde and Benjamin Araya during the 2003 Copa Cámara de Diputados final, Palermo.

Benjamin is the oldest of the Araya clan. His brothers say: 'He was and is the best of all of us!' Benjamin won the Argentine Open with his father Horacio in 1983, aged twenty. In fact he has won the Open three times in total. He is also the youngest player ever to win the Open; he was only seventeen years old when he won it in 1980. Juan Carlos Harriot and Horacio Heguy had both decided to retire from the Coronel Suárez team and Benjamin filled one of those places. At the time the team didn't expect to win at their first attempt, but they did.

Here in the Cámara he is on another Araya homebred mare called Serenata.

Lucas Monteverde has been a professional polo player since the age of seventeen. 'I love horses and I love sport, so I ended up playing polo.' In 1997 Lucas won the Sotogrande Gold Cup, and in 1995 he won the Deauville Gold Cup. Back in Argentina, he won the Cámara de Diputados two years in a row: 2002 and 2003. In 2003 he also won the Jockey Club trophy with Adolfo Cambiaso, Lolo Castagnola and Pancho Bensadon.

'My true ambition is to win the Open! Polo is definitely a way of life. It is also the only thing I can do: breeding horses and playing polo. I love life on the farm!'

Santiago Araya (the second oldest of the four Araya brothers), Coronel Suárez, in a ride-off against Alejandro Agote, El Paraiso, during the 2003 Copa Cámara de Diputados semi-final, Palermo.

Brother Pepe describes Santiago as 'the fighter'.

'Santiago works really hard for the team and he never gives up on any play. He is the pivotal figure in our team.'

Santiago runs a business renting out machines for construction in Buenos Aires and only plays polo at weekends now. He used to play for Rick Stowe, patron of Geebung, for eight years, after which he went into business with Rick. 'I enjoy it very much. We have an office in Buenos Aires and I live in Pilar where I play at my farm as well as playing during the polo season.

'I don't travel to play polo anymore but I keep as fit as I can and work at my game in order to be as professional as possible. This is hard during our winter because I can only play at weekends, but it is the European summer at this time and everybody is in Europe competing hard. Come September when all the Argentine professionals come back for Palermo, they are in full swing while I am trying to fit in! Playing for Coronel Suárez is tough because they have done so well in the history of polo. To beat that record is practically impossible, but every time you put the Coronel Suárez shirt on you sweat to get a good result.

'I enjoy playing with my brothers and I think that it's only because I play with them that I am still playing. We are the only team that really practically solely plays on horses we have bred on our farm.

'Here I am on my best and favourite horse, Ranita. She was voted Champion of Champions in a ridden showing class out of 200 polo ponies! For us as a family, polo means everything! I just love horses! My wife once asked me who I preferred, my best polo mare or her? Well, I told her not to ask such dangerous questions!'

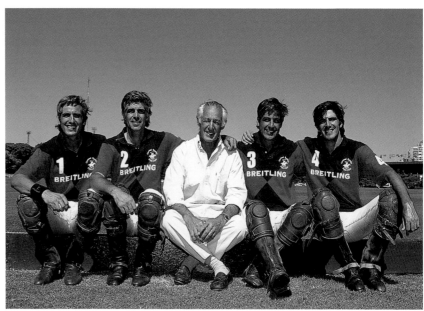

Five times Araya. This time not all are brothers; father Horacio sneaked in amongst his sons!

Polo really runs through the Arayas' veins. The boys' grandfather played polo and although he was not a great player, he was very enthusiastic, and so his passion for the game filtered all the way down to his grandsons, and possibly even further.

Pepe Araya tells us more. 'My father took polo more seriously when he moved to Coronel Suárez, the centre of polo in those days. He was really fanatical about polo and he still plays today at fifty-seven, but off five now. He reached handicap nine at forty-six, and he won the Argentine Open with my brother Benjamin in 1983.

'Coronel Suárez is the name of a town with a polo club. It is situated about 550 kilometres from Buenos Aires. It is a very important club and possibly the best-known club in Argentina. It has seven polo grounds, tennis courts and a golf course. The Arayas lived in that town and grew up playing polo at the club.

'The most famous Coronel Suárez team was when the two Heguys and the two Harriots represented their club; that group won the Argentine Open seventeen times. Coronel Suárez won it a total of twenty-five times.

'For us Araya brothers it is a real pleasure and honour to be representing Coronel Suárez. Playing for the club enables us to give the club something in return for all it has given us over the years and when we grew up.'

Antony Fanshawe captained England at the 2003 European Championships in Dallas Burston.

Antony has been playing polo for twenty years, but he comes from a racing and hunting background and only started playing polo at the relatively late age of twenty. These were the third European Championships at which he competed. These photos were taken at the two matches when England played Italy. The photo of Agustin Nero, on the grey, marking Antony was taken during the league match; the other was taken during the final.

'We were not really playing as a team in that first match. Italy played much better than us; they *were* a team, and so we ended up losing! However, losing was either going to make or break us as a team and would determine how we progressed in the remainder of the tournament. Fortunately we had already qualified for the semis before this match. A good talk with our coach Claire Tomlinson

helped too. Claire is a great coach and a great person. You can tell her the truth and she will give the truth back, which is very important and essential for building a good team.'

When England met Italy again, this time in the final, they had ironed out their differences.

'Coming into the final, we had already played very well against Spain in the semi-final. This had given us a good feeling and helped us regain respect for one another. Italy never really got close to us this time. We were very focused and ran away with the first two chukkas. The ball broke for us a lot, which was lucky, but we also took and converted our chances. As the captain, I was under a lot of pressure because England had never lost the European zone. Luckily the more pressure we were under, the better we played! Polo is an impossible sport to be consistent in without discipline! Trying to find perfection as a player or in a horse is fascinating. One could almost say that a passion could easily become an obsession.'

Argentine Matias MacDonough played the eighteen-goal Ellerston tournament in March 2004 for Ellerston with his cousin Gonzalito Pieres. Also on the team were Johnny Williams and Andrew Blake Thomas. In the final they met and beat Wastecorp.

'Ellerston is amazing. A great, great place! It was my first year there in 2004. I started playing for Ellerstina in Argentina at the 2003 Open with my brother Pablo and the two Piereses. The Piereses have played for Ellerston for a long time and it was Gonzalito who invited me to play in Ellerston. We are very good friends. Some of the players were busy in Florida so Gonzalito and I ended up going to Ellerston. Gonzalito is a hell of a player and playing with him was a really good experience. The horses in Ellerston are really fabulous, some of them truly amazing, and proof of the quality of their breeding programme.'

Matias MacDonough about to put his whole body into a backhand during the 2004 semi-final Gold Cup match at Cowdray. Graff Capital lost 12–17 to Dubai.

Matias turned professional at seventeen. In 1987 he got a job playing for Brunei for ten years. He first travelled to England in 1992 as a Brunei player and has been coming here since then. Matias names his biggest victories.

'Winning the 2001 Copa Cámara de Diputados in Argentina with my brother. I lost a few semis at the Open itself yet I still rate these matches as being some of my finest matches. I also won the Coronation Cup in 2000. However, I still think that playing the Open is what it's all about. It's just a completely different story.

'Polo means a lot to me and I'm already thinking ahead because I know that my career as a player will not go on forever. No medicine will come to my rescue, time is time! I am, therefore, preparing myself for that moment and it means that I'm working on strengthening my business skills. My interest in breeding horses is growing ever stronger too. It is a learning curve because you could be breeding for thirty years and still be discovering the wonders of it. I want to do my best and I have already had some success with my broodmares, but my ultimate goal is to become the best breeder in the whole of Argentina! I have also become a father and I would like to have a big family. All this needs adjusting to as well. Coming back to my short-term goal, that, of course, is still to win as many big events as I can, while I can.'

Santiago Gaztambide playing for
Il Macereto in a league match for
The Challenge Cup, Cowdray 2003.
Taking all sorts of precautions is
Australian Glen Gilmore, playing
for Groeninghe.

'Santi' started to ride at the
age of three. He has been a
professional polo player for twenty
years and is a regular visitor to
England. He has played the
Argentine Open for many years and
reached the finals twice.

'I'm hitting a neck shot
because one of my team-mates is
coming for the pass. Glen is
covering himself because it seems
that he is a bit too close for
comfort, but he had nothing to
fear. This shot is not half as
difficult as the nearside shot under
the neck.

'Polo is a fantastic combination
of pleasure and business while
being in touch with horses. It's one
of the best things one could be
doing. I live on a farm in Argentina
where we breed horses. My father
started it all but I have also
started taking an interest in
breeding; it's all part of the
preparation for giving me
something to do in my old age!'

Glen describes his side of what
went on in the shot.

'I was just worried because I
was on such a small horse; she
belongs to my patron, Isabel. She
is tiny, only about 14.3 hh, and I
thought to myself that when
Santi with his long arms is hitting
a neck shot, I might just get hit
in the face. I was covering
everything up; my leg is up and
I'm cringing. My God, I look
stupid; oh well, that's the way it
goes!'

(Opposite and above) Dario Musso playing for HB in the 2003 Deauville Gold Cup semi-final against Grassfield.

Dario is from Córdoba, Argentina, and has been playng in Europe since 1995, mainly in France, Belgium and Italy. He has been playing in Deauville since 1999 and loves it there.

'I know a lot of lovely people in Deauville and when I am there I always play for the HB team of the Pailloncy family. They are great and we have a lot of fun. In 2003 we won the fourteen-goal Silver Cup before going on to win the Gold Cup itself. We were already over the moon about winning the Silver Cup, especially as it had been the first fourteen-goal match Sébastien and Ludovic Pailloncy had ever won. We had a bet going that if we won it we would shave our heads, and so the two brothers, Ignacio Tillous, eight grooms and I shaved our heads!'

This probably brough HB luck for the twenty-goal Gold Cup, for which Dario joined forces with Mark Tomlinson, Ernesto Trotz and the Pailloncy brothers, who took it in turns to play.

'The match against Grassfield was very important as the winner went through to the final. I remember it being a very tight and physical match, and we only won thanks to a goal by Mark in extra time. Beating Royal Barrière in the final was down to our horses being fresher than theirs. We were able to save our horses' energy a little in the match against Talandracas, which meant we had more horsepower for the final. We also did a good job of marking Marcos Heguy that day.

'Winning both cups with HB in the same year was amazing; it was crazy and, as you can imagine, we had quite a party!'

(Opposite and above) Argentine Ignacio Tillous playing for Grassfield in the 2003 Gold Cup semi-final in Deauville agains HB.

Ignacio, from Córdoba, Argentina, became a professional player at sixteen, and is a seven-goal player when competing in Deauville. He first travelled to Atlantic City as a three-goal player and was put up to five at nineteen. Since then Ignacio has played all over Europe, mainly in Italy, Spain, France, Belgium, Holland and Switzerland. In 2004 Ignacio played in Gstaad for Swiss patron Pierre Genecand and the Mirasol team. He regularly competes in tournaments on snow; in St. Moritz, playing for Bank Hofmann, Ignacio won the Cartier Trophy in 2003. The same year he also won the Deauville Silver Cup when playing for HB.

'Playing against HB in the Gold Cup when I actually played, and won, the Silver Cup with them only a few days before, was a funny feeling, especially as I am great friends with Dario Musso. In polo you can be team-mates one minute and opponents the next. I enjoyed playing with the Pailloncy brothers, Ludovic and Sébastien, they learn fast and are constantly improving. That day my ex-team-mates got the better of us in the semis. It was a tough match and we lost by just one goal in extra time. Losing a semi-final is always a very emotional experience. However, I really enjoyed playing in Deauville; I love the town, it's really pretty and the atmosphere is great too. To have the polo grounds in the centre of Deauville racecourse is quite special; sometimes a race would be going on around us!'

In 1995 Ignacio won the twenty-goal Gold Cup in Bogota, Bolivia. He also won the Campanionato Argentino del Interior four times.

'Polo became a passion when I was thirteen. My father loves the sport; we have a farm in Córdoba where we breed horses and he always gives good players horses to play the Argentine Open. He is also a great supporter of my polo.'

Juan Martin Nero, Azzurra, pulling up his mount after realizing
that Carlos Gracida, Labegorce, is just about to turn away from
him to take the ball into the opposite direction during the
2004 Queen's Cup final.

Carlos's ultimate target during the 2004 high-goal season in
England was to finally win this highly desirable trophy.

'Trying to win the Queen's Cup was a big challenge for me. I
wanted to win it so badly and, somehow, deep inside, I did
believe that 2004 was going to be the year. I had, after all,
been in the final, as well as getting really close to winning it,
countless times. When I finally did it, I was overjoyed. It was
like a big relief!'

Carlos Gracida executing a wonderful under-the-neck shot in the direction of the goal during the 2003 Gold Cup quarter-final match between Labegorce and Oakland Park.

'I remember this play well. It was the end of the game in the sixth chukka. We were leading by two goals when I hit this under-the-neck shot. It was one of those rare moments where you don't want to score, you just want to hit the ball out of play. So, although I was aiming in the direction of the goal, I wasn't really trying to score because I knew that Oakland Park was not able to come back at this stage.

'I'm on Oakley an English thoroughbred mare I bought in England. She had also played the US Open. After the Gold Cup final, however, she actually went lame with an injury to her knee and, sadly, she has not played polo since.'

Miguel Novillo-Astrada, Graffham, on board Chita, and Carlos Gracida, Labegorce, on Polvosa, during the 2003 Veuve Cliquot Gold Cup semi-final.

Carlos recalls how the match was won.

'We were losing by three goals and suddenly I got my confidence back: that magic I used to have when I managed to win games even when trailing by three or four goals. Graffham were a very strong team that year. Out of ten matches we would probably have lost nine, but I knew we could win that day and it really counted! During that match I dug deeper than I have ever done in my entire career. After the match I was mentally and physically exhausted. I had never tried harder to win than during that semi-final. I was also on my best horse, Polvosa. I can't really explain how it happened, I just felt that my magic was back and it was a great feeling. Certain things happen and it's like everything is moving in slow motion: you are still going flat

out but you seem to be thinking faster than the game! Perhaps being on Polvosa helped; she has speed and stamina, and I love the way she turns. I bought her as a yearling from the sales in Ocala, Florida. She is by a famous stallion called General Assembly who was sold to Japan for 22 million dollars! I usually play her in chukkas two and six.'

Miguel only remembers that his team played really well that match.

'Gillian had a really good game. In a way we were a touch unlucky but, to be truthful, I think that Labegorce was the better team. I was trying to win the position by riding-off Carlos to prevent him from hitting the shot. I can't really remember what happened next. Chita is very fast but maybe she wasn't quite fast enough at that moment!'

Mexican Carlos Gracida playing for Catamount during the 2004 US Open quarter-final.

For this match American ten-goal player Mike Azzaro was suffering with back pain and was replaced by Adolfo Cambiaso. Other team-mates were Scott Devon and fellow Mexican Pelon Escapite. Catamount was facing Gillian Johnston's team, Bendabout, with Adam Snow and brothers Miguel and Alejandro Novillo-Astrada as Gillian's team-mates.

'I managed to escape although Adam is still close to me. I'm on Decada a young, first-season mare. She is a little big for a polo pony but nevertheless she has all the potential to become a real champion. She arrived from Mexico in January and was playing the US Open in April;

only a very few horses in the world can do that! I scored from this play! We ended up beating Bendabout 10–4.

'Adam Snow is a very professional player. He is very dedicated and always trying to find new ways to improve his concentration. I think he is into yoga.'

American Adam snow became a professional player in 1988 when playing off five goals.

'My first trip abroad was when Australian Bernard Roux sent me a ticket to play the Melbourne Cup, which we won, beating Kerry Packer and Ellerston. After the match Bernard gave me 500 dollars and sent me to a clothes shop. I bought clothes there that I still wear today.

'Playing the US Open is always special. It is the biggest tournament of the season for me. Losing the quarter-finals in 2004 gave me a pain in my gut because we had the team to win that game. Cambiaso replacing Azzaro was a psychological burden for us and Carlos did play very well that day. I am on my mare Pumbaa; I named her after the character in *The Lion King*. She won Best Playing Pony at the US Open in 2002, which we won with Gillian Johnston when her team was called Coca Cola. Winning meant a lot to me that year because I went from a nine-goal player to ten.'

When I caught up with Adam, he was in Argentina.

'John Goodman, patron of Isla Carroll, sponsored a team to compete in Argentina. Together with fellow American Jeff Hall, South African Sugar Erskine and Argentine Gaston Laulhe, we played the qualifiers and are now competing in the Hurlingham and the Open itself. I played the Open before, in 1999, but this time, 2004, I brought my own horses, which makes a big difference. In fact, thanks to John, we brought a total of eighteen horses over.

'Polo is what gives me excitement and makes me feel alive.'

Javier Novillo-Astrada, Black Bears, with an under-the-neck shot past Simon Keyte, Foxcote, during the 2004 Warwickshire Cup final.

Although Simon works for Urs Schwarzenbach almost all year round, when he is in England for the high-goal season he doesn't play for Black Bears.

'The mix of playing for Garangula during the European winter months and yet being able to come and play in Europe for their season is great. I think it is what saves me from going mad! Garangula is almost stress free because Rowan George is managing things. There my only concerns are to make sure the horses are right for us and to play the best I can. When I'm in England, however, I help the guys with the fourteen horses for Urs, and I have a dozen of my own horses in livery at the Black Bears' set-up in Shiplake, and I play for other patrons' teams, like Tony Pidgley's Cadenza or the Vesteys' Foxcote.'

Getting wind of horses that would make great polo ponies is not always easy. Rowan George, manager of Urs Schwarzenbach's farm, Garangula, is always on the look-out for them.

Shimmer, the grey Javier is on, is a very well-bred mare from new Zealand that Rowan found in 1999. She is by All Glory, a Group One winner in New Zealand, and out of Ikantango, a winner of three races. Her full brother won three races in Hong Kong. Prior to her polo career, Shimmer was called Steal Your Thunder, a name under which she won a six-furlong race in New Zealand. When she went to Australia, Simon Keyte played her in the winning Garangula sixteen-goal team at Ellerston in March 1999. The top horses from Garangula travel to England for the high-goal seasons, and so Shimmer travelled over in May 1999 and has played consistently for Black Bears since 2000, except for the year of the foot-and-mouth epidemic. She has won a few Best Playing Pony awards; the Gold Cup in 2002 – which Black Bears won – being one of them. It is no wonder she is one of Javier's favourite horses.

Memo Gracida, Isla Carroll, on the ball just ahead of Sebastian Merlos, Lechuza, who is trying to hook Memo during the 2004 US Open semi-final in Wellington, Florida.

Memo's relationship with the US Open is very special for many reasons.

'The US Open is so important to me primarily because it is the first polo tournament I saw outside Mexico in 1975, and you have all the history that goes with the US Open. Because it was the 100th anniversary, 2004 was unique and I had not won the title for six years. Also, I was part of all the thinking that went in to creating the club here where the Open was played. All this added another dimension to my emotions. The great trust John Goodman put in me also touched me; it was a real vote of confidence on his part. I always prepare myself very well for the US Open but, to tell you the truth, we were actually the underdogs because I had not won it for so many years and because neither Pancho Bensadon nor Sugar Erskine, although very good players, had ever won the title. But we all worked hard and were able to pull it off.'

Mexican Memo Gracida, polo player *par excellence*, and certainly one of the all-time greats, executing a defensive shot during the 2004 US Open final.

Memo, playing for Isla Carroll, with patron John  Goodman, Sugar Erskine and Pancho Bensadon, secured his sixteenth US Open title by defeating White Birch 10–6. After the match Memo described the game.

'White Birch were very quick and very accurate in the beginning. At half-time we were one goal ahead which gave us confidence, but I told my team-mates that we were not playing our best. OK, we were one goal ahead but this doesn't mean much in polo. It was important that we kept working hard for the next three chukkas. And we did; the team worked very well.'

Memo, forty-seven in 2004, proved to be as sharp as ever. He has incredible vision, superb field awareness, near-to-perfect ball control and, on this day, demonstrated over and over again how to play to the strength of one's team-mates.

Memo has been playing off a ten-goal handicap for well over twenty years and his horsemanship is second to none. It is no wonder that he has been, and still is, a role model for many polo players around the world.

For younger brother by four years, Carlos Gracida, Memo was simply the inspiration that made him want to be a professional polo player too. Together they have won the US Open seven times.

'I love playing with my brother Memo. I mean, his record speaks for itself. He is one of the all-time greats! And to top it all, he is my brother! What more can you ask for than to play with him!

For Memo: 'Winning the US titles with Carlos was really special too. He is the best team-mate I have ever had in my polo career and I feel very lucky to have had him. Carlos is very talented. A complete player and team-mate, particularly in the forward position. We just complement each other very well!'

Pepe Araya on his homebred mare Amistad leading the field in the 2003 Jack Gannon Cup final, a subsidiary of the Veuve Cliquot Gold Cup, between Graff Capital and Cowdray.

'This was the first time I played for Markus Graff and I enjoyed meeting him. We didn't win but nonetheless it was an enjoyable game.

'All in all I would say that I prefer breeding and training young horses to playing the game itself, but I need to play as well to make a living from polo. My dream is to have my own farm, breed horses and school youngsters.

'Polo is an important part of my life. I literally play all year round. To give you an example, I have only had one week's holiday since I got married nine years ago. You could say that polo has taken over my life!'

Australian Robert Ballard is heading the field and getting ready to unleash a massive forehand in Australia's league match against the USA in the F.I.P. World Championships, Chantilly, September 2004.

Robert plays off a four-goal handicap and is based at James Ashton's Millamolong Polo Station. Robert played for Millamolong Yellow at Ellerston earlier that same year.

'I got the polo bug as a kid! I love working with horses and my biggest thrill is training young horses and getting them to play good polo. Sitting on an animal that is going that fast and hitting a little ball around is just unbelievable!'

In their first match of the tournament, Australia played France and with the score standing at 11–2 in favour of France, they hadn't really got off to a good start.

'We couldn't have played any worse than the way in which we had played France! When playing the USA we pulled together as a team and tried really hard. We couldn't finish off a few goals and the USA finished off pretty much every goal-scoring chance they had, which meant that we lost that match 12–7.

'However, it's been amazing and playing against so many different players has just been a great experience! Riding different horses, difficult or nice ones, and getting around and meeting all these new people has been fun. Of course you always prefer your own horses without a doubt but riding horses you're not used to is all part of the challenge. It's true, you just don't know what the horses are going to be like or under which rider they will go best and that adds to the excitement.'

Team USA was in the same group as Australia, France and Chile. In this photo (left), Steve Orothwein is trying to hit the ball while France's Brieux Rigaux is laying all his horse's weight against him. In the second shot (above), USA's Jason Crowder is not really being challenged.

Steve Crowder, USA team coach, summed up their performance.

'In the game with France we only won one chukka and, by that time, we were behind too much. We had opportunities but we missed too many chances in front of goal. We controlled the ball, we just didn't control the scoring! France played well. We took a gamble in the last chukka by not taking the man but by just running to the ball. That worked but, to be fair, the French were also on their worst horses in the sixth chukka. It was too late, however; we had already gotten into trouble early in the match.

'Against Australia, we played well. I believe they had a weak team and they definitely drew the worst group of horses.

'The horses were fair. We drew horses from Spain. I would have to say that they were not fit enough. People think that for a fourteen-goal tournament horses don't have to be all that fit but these kids are hard running and the level of play was stronger than it usually is at fourteen-goal matches.'

(Right and far right)
Chantilly 2004.

One of the English team's
polo ponies, Chantilly 2004.
Ponies carry identifying
numbers so that judges can
control the amount of time
they play, which should be
no more than seven minutes
a match.

(Opposite) Renato Diniz-Junqueira on the ball ahead of
Andrew Blake Thomas in the 2004 F.I.P. World Championships
final, Chantilly 2004.

After England beat Chile in the semi-final, Andrew was full
of hope.

'Being in the final feels pretty good. I am very excited and
happy to be there! We would like to play Brazil in the final
as we only just lost to them by one goal in our first match.'

Andrew's wish came true. England met Brazil again in the
final. This time the match went into overtime and England
didn't quite manage to pull it off.

Renato's wish also came true. At the beginning of the
tournament he stated that his biggest ambition was to win
the 2004 World Championship for his country!

(Top) England captain Tom Morley with an under-the-neck shot in the F.I.P. World Championships final, Chantilly, September 2004, followed by Luis Diniz-Junqueira, Brazil, a three-goal player and the older brother of Renato, showing his determination.

Tom was the only player remaining from the England team that won the European Zone enabling England to qualify for these World Championships.

'Brazil was a very strong and good team. I think we showed a lot of composure to be able to draw level with them in the sixth. The match was very close and the seventh chukka could have gone either way. It was the most enjoyable game of polo I have ever played on a competitive level as well as from a sportsmanship point of view. There was no animosity, no malice. It was a lot quicker too because every player was able to hit the ball equally well which did not allow for errors. You had to anticipate more quickly because, if you didn't, the other team was sure to score. Playing four-man polo is a great way of playing. Luis was a really good player and very difficult to mark. The Brazilian player who stood out for me was their number three, their captain, Caloa de Mello. He played with such passion and kept his team under control.'

(Middle) Matt Lodder on the offensive for England with Brazilian Paique Ganon in pursuit.

(Bottom) Loose ball up in the air. Matt Lodder overshot it and Luis Diniz-Junqueira is trying to reach for it.

(Opposite) Renato Diniz-Junqueira is about to make contact with the ball while his marker, James Harper, respecting the rules, can only look on.

James started playing polo with the West Sussex Pony Club at the age of thirteen. Presently James is playing off a five-goal handicap; his biggest ambition is to become one of the best English players and to represent his country on Cartier International Day. After taking the semi-final match from Chile, he spoke of having to concentrate on getting the horses right for the final.

'We drew pretty OK horses and all the teams were pretty even.'

This Chantilly F.I.P. World Championships final was an incredible match. It went into a seventh, golden-goal chukka and England coach Claire Tomlinson summed up what happened.

'Our boys did really well! They came back from two goals down in the last chukka to level the match and take it into a deciding seventh chukka with the golden-goal rule. We had a big mix up and long wait before the seventh chukka which wasn't helpful. At first, no one was quite clear about which horses the players were allowed to ride as the horses were only allowed to play a maximum of seven minutes per match. The muddle resulted in a bit of a nightmare. However, when the match finally resumed, it could have gone either way. Brazil had a bit of luck on their side as they got away with committing a couple of fouls against us, which were not given. All in all, the boys did really well. In fact they played well throughout the tournament. Getting used to playing what we call four-man polo, i.e playing without a patron, was very difficult for our boys. It's a much faster game but they adapted really well.'

Calao de Mello, captain of the Brazilian team during the F.I.P World Championships, Chantilly 2004.

Once the golden goal was scored in favour of Brazil, the entire team fell off their horses, collapsed, and ended up in a heap one on top of the other! The Brazilians were over the moon and could not believe what they had just accomplished! Nothing could stop them from acting out scenes we regularly witness on a football pitch!

Captain Calao described it thus.

'This win means a lot! It is the result of real good teamwork. We worked on having a great relationship and we set ourselves a target. This, I think, helped us to focus and to pull it off.

'The final was the toughest match of the tournament. England was definitely the toughest team to beat. They were very professional and have a great coach in Claire Tomlinson.

Brazil was a young team and we believed in ourselves. We spent weekends together and built a strong bond. I truly believe that it was meant to be! We had two chances to lose the game. England too lost two sure chances to score and win!

I really asked God for guidance and I would have accepted losing just like I accepted a win. I put my trust in God and had the confidence that the right thing would happen. I said to God, "if we lose, please show us the way to get better".

'I am not overly religious but I do believe in energy and love. I love my father; he used to breed horses and he loved polo. He died eight years ago. I talked to him a lot during the final. I felt and knew that he was by my side when I missed the penalty as well as when we received the trophy!

'I have great respect for all the English players. Especially for my counterpart, Tom Morley. We played a clean game and played with respect. Before we went into the seventh chukka I told Tom that we were friends before the match and that no matter the outcome, we would be friends again once the match was over. Tom agreed and we shook hands.'

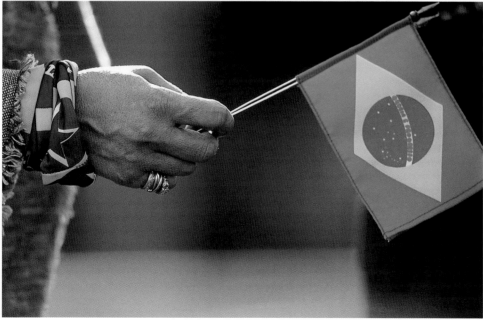

Gaetan Charloux and Renato Diniz-Junqueira during the semi-final between France and Brazil in the 2004 F.I.P. World Championships, Chantilly.

Brazil's captain Calao de Mello celebrated his team's effort, happy to have made it through to the final.

'We really concentrated on that match. Prior to our encounter we spent six hours studying their play: we studied their horses and the tactics they adopted in their previous matches. I believe that this helped us to win the match by nine goals to four.'

Brazilian supporter, Chantilly 2004.

Pablo Spinacci, Labegorce, and Sebastian Dawnay, Black Bears, during a league match for the 2004 Gold Cup. The match was played at Anningsley Park, home of Labegorce.

Pablo had the misfortune of breaking his mallet, while Sebastian is possibly trying to get to cover? But what I want to know is, which ball is Pablo aiming at?

James Packer, son of the one and only Kerry Packer: a man the polo world owes a lot to.

Here James is playing for Ellerston in the final of the 2003 Garangula Tournament against the home team, Garangula. He is riding Cabernet, a result of the embryo transfer breeding programme at Ellerston. Cabernet progressed through the Ellerston training programme and gets played by different Ellerston players. Amongst other wins, James was part of the Ellerston White team that won the 12–16-goal Ellerston Challenge Cup. Also in the team were his good friend John Williams, David Stirling and Gonzalito Pieres.

Mexican Carlos Gracida, Labegorce, and Argentine Miguel Novillo-Astrado, Graffham, fighting for the ball during the hotly contested 2003 Gold Cup semi-final at Cowdray Park. Pepe Heguy, Labegorce, is attempting to ride-off Miguel, while Tommy Fernandez-Llorente, Graffham, is following at close range.

Carlos recalls how both emotionally and mentally draining playing that match had been. Graffham were leading by three goals and yet, thanks to Carlos's magic and fighting spirit, Labegorce won the match.

'I like to consider myself a winner, no matter which team I happen to be playing for. The challenge is always to be competitive and to win. This match was no different. I gave it my best; I kept believing that we could come back and win, and fortunately we did!'

(Clockwise from right)
Santiago Chavanne (Arg).
Fred Mannix (Can).
Stefano Marsaglia (It).
Pite Merlos (Arg).
Pelon Escapite (Mex).

PORTRAITS

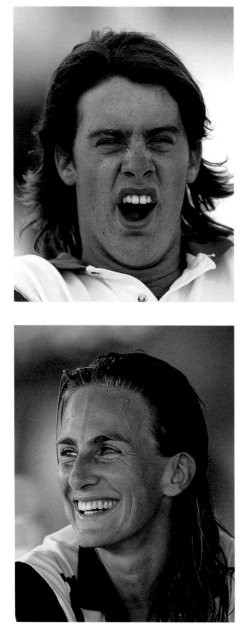

(Clockwise from above)
Celine Charloux (Fr).
Facundo Pieres (Arg).
Mike Azzaro (USA).
Eduardo Novillo-Astrada (Arg).
Alejandro 'Piki' Diaz-Alberdi (Arg).

(Clockwise from right)
Adolfo Cambiaso (Arg).
Gonzalito Pieres (Arg).
Milo Fernandez-Araujo (Arg).
Alejandro 'Negro' Novillo-Astrada (Arg).
Marcos Heguy (Arg).

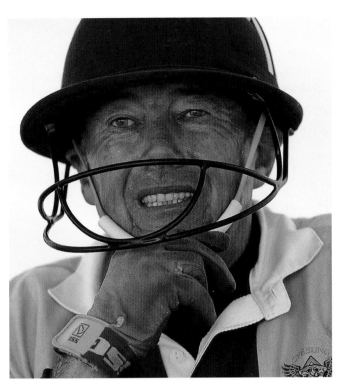

(Clockwise from left)
Rick Stowe (Australia).
Mariano Aguerre (Arg).
Bautista Heguy (Arg).
James Packer (Australia).
Horacio Heguy (Arg).

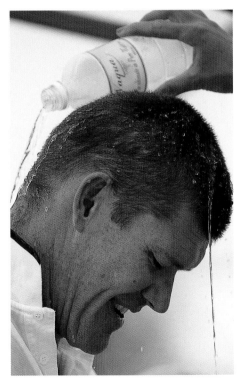

(Clockwise from left)
Matt Lodder (Eng).
Bartolomé 'Lolo' Castagnola (Arg).
Urs Schwarzenbach (Switz).
Pierre Henry Ngoumou (Fr).
Miguel Novillo-Astrada (Arg).

(Clockwise from below)
Viare Antinori (Arg).
Adam Snow (USA).
Gerardo 'Toto' Collardin (Arg).
Sven Schneider (Ger).
John Paul 'JP' Clarkin (NZ).

(Clockwise from below)
Alberto 'Pepe' Heguy (Arg).
Sebastian Dawnay (Ire).
Dario Musso (Arg).
Roger Carlsson (Sw).
Guillermo 'Memo' Gracida (Mex).

(Clockwise from left)
Tariq Albwardi (Dub).
Carlos Gracida (Mex).
Jaime Huidobro (Chile).
Pablo Mora (Sp).
Ignacio 'Nacho' Domecq (Sp).

A very emotional Brazilian team could hardly contain their joy after beating England in overtime for the 2004 World Championship title.

Captain Luis Carlos 'Calao' de Mello puts their win down to really good teamwork.

'We worked on having a great relationship and we set ourselves a target. This, I believe, helped us to focus and to pull it off. The final was the toughest match of the tournament because we had to beat the most dangerous team; England had great players and a great coach in Claire Tomlinson. We were a young team and we believed in ourselves. I truly feel that our win was meant to be because on two occasions we should have lost the game. England didn't take advantage of two sure chances to score and win, so didn't.'

WINNING MOMENTS

Emma Tomlinson, Satnam Dhillon, Pepe Araya and Santiago Gaztambide entered the 2004 Gold Cup tournament as the Beaufort team. In a great match against Talandracas they won the Ashton Silver Cup, a subsidiary of the Gold Cup, 11–10.

In the quarter-finals of the Gold Cup itself, the Beaufort lost a very exciting match to Graff Capital in extra time, and Satnam pointed out certain truths.

'You make your own destiny in a match and if you miss an open goal and a thirty-yard penalty all in the last minute of the sixth chukka, you can't come off the field as winners! Winning the Ashton Silver Cup, however, was good, especially as our team for the Gold Cup tournament was put together at the very last minute.'

(Right) The Rest of the Commonwealth team, comprising Canadian Fred Mannix, Australian Rookie Baillieu, New Zealander Simon Keyte and Australian Glen Gilmore, beat England by just one goal to win the prestigious 2002 Coronation Cup.

Simon Keyte recalls the match.

'I would have to say that winning that day was the best feeling I have ever had in polo! We never thought we were going to win. We thought we'd give England a run for their money but we never imagined we would be able to pull it off. We won within thirty seconds of regular time. The ball hit my mare and went in! Rookie was playing out of his skin; and Freddie, playing at one, was phenomenal! Glen and I play together a lot and had a good understanding that day too. England is always exeptionally well mounted on Cartier Day but our horsepower was great as well.

'Before going down to the presentation, we all gave each other a big hug but actually it had not quite sunk in. Glen and I just kept repeating in disbelief "we have just won that!"'

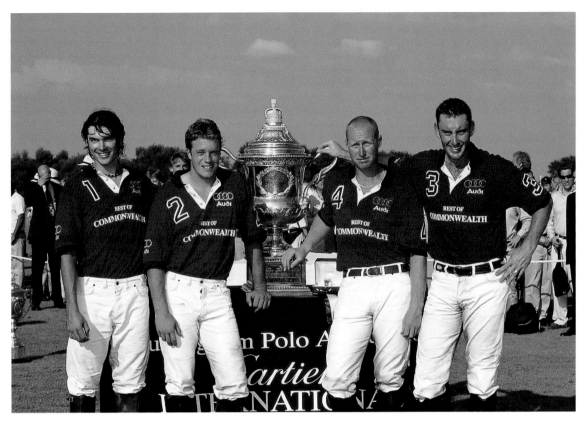

(Above) The prestigious Coronation Cup in its full glory. It is, no doubt, the cup every team captain wants to get his hands on!

(Left) Glen Gilmore captained The Rest of The Commonwealth team for the 2002 Coronation Cup at Guards Polo Club.

He absolutely loves playing on Cartier Day. In 1999 he even played with two pins in an ankle he broke six weeks prior to the match because: 'I wasn't going to miss playing on this amazing stage for anything in the world.'

'In 2002 I was actually fit and this time we won by one goal!' Glen could not contain his joy and managed to lift this amazing trophy single-handedly! 'It is a seriously heavy trophy and I was told afterwards that I had been the first player to lift it above their head!'

In 2003 England had a happier encounter on Cartier Day than the previous year. Henry Brett, Andrew Hine, Luke Tomlinson and Will Lucas beat the Mexican 'family' team of Memo, Carlos and Reubens Gracida and Roberto Gonzalez.

Andrew Hine took over as England captain in 1999 after Howard Hipwood retired, and rates beating Mexico in the 2003 Coronation Cup as one of his fondest memories as England captain. Although Andrew might have surprised a few by retiring as captain after that match, he believes that it was a great way to finish.

'Memo and Carlos Gracida are great icons of British polo and we went into the match thinking we would get a big thumping. We were really not the bookmakers' choice! Also, I had always said to myself that forty would be a good age to retire. Had we *not* won I might have stayed on, but because it did go our way I felt very comfortable with my decision.

'Playing for your country is the most amazing feeling! When the commentator invited me, as the captain of the winning team, to come forward to receive the cup, a tingle went down my spine and I picked up the cup, which incidentally weighs a ton! It is just so very special.'

Henry Brett, who was to take on the captaincy of England in 2004, remembers the moment.

'Winning in front of a huge crowd as well as winning for your country is always an amazing feeling. The Coronation Cup is a one-off game so it's not as emotional an event as winning a big tournament when you have worked all that time to qualify for the final. The bottom line, however, has got to be that it's always good to win, especially as I don't like losing!'

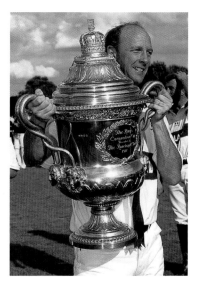

In 2004 Chile was invited to play England on Cartier Day. Brothers Gabriel and José Donoso, Jaime Huidobro and Alejandro Vial were the stronger team on the day and beat brothers Luke and Mark Tomlinson, their cousin Will Lucas and newly appointed England captain Henry Brett.

Gabriel Donoso captained the Chilean team.

'Winning the Coronation Cup mattered much more to me than just the fact that Chile was playing England. It was like taking on a very important commitment! I am so glad that we pulled it off because, personally, I felt a lot of pressure playing at that level. My game never felt good during the entire season, so I wanted to prove to myself that I could still compete and play well at that level. That day we played against four young England players who were especially well mounted for the Coronation Cup. We managed with lesser horses, and horses are the key factor of the game, and so I am very proud of that too because we really got the most out of our horses.'

Younger brother José Donoso was just as excited.

'Cartier Day is a hugely important day! It is amazing and one of the best feelings you experience as a polo player. Everybody you love comes to support you.'

José converted vital penalties and had this explanation.

'During the 2004 season I played two games for Broncos where I had a 100 per cent success rate when hitting my penalties, which is by no means usual for me as I am not a great penalty hitter! So I thought of saving that mallet for a special day. I didn't play with it for two months and only brought it out today where it did its magic again!'

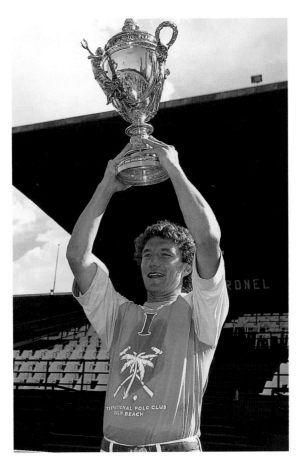

(Left) A proud moment for South African Sugar Erskine, IPC, Palm Beach.

Together with Lucas Monteverde, Gastón Laulhé and Marcos di Paola he won the 2003 Copa Cámara de Diputados in Palermo, Argentina.

Sugar first travelled to Argentina in 1993. In 2002 he reached the semi-final of the Cámara when his team lost to La Mariana in overtime.

'It is not easy to get to the US, let alone Argentina, as a player from South Africa. Back home we were more like weekend warriors. The professional aspect of how polo was played in the US and Argentina blew me away. The Cámara was always a tournament I used to watch others play, and to be winning it myself was so unexpected and just amazing. I love the way polo is played in Argentina; it's always very evenly matched. They play the purest polo. Matches are usually very tight and are won by only one or two goals. The deadlock does not affect the play. It's heartfelt polo – emotions run high. Winning is a dream come true.

'I just followed my father's suggestion to go to Argentina, and here I am doing what every polo player dreams of: playing big tournaments in Argentina. I find it quite hard to live my dream. It's like walking on untrodden ground. When I wake up I have to pinch myself in order to believe that I am actually in Argentina and playing at the top level.

'I just love the sport; polo is my life but I can't say that it is down to the horses – it is something else deep inside, and I can't really put my finger on it. My father was a great influence although neither of my parents ever pushed me, or my brother and sister, into anything in particular; they let us go our own way, which inspired me to do something I love. I can say that my dad gave me the opportunity to love something that was inside me. My parents are both very free-spirited and they brought us up with that free spirit.

For me, polo is war with a smile (my dad always told me to smile); I go about it in a professional manner but I don't take it too seriously.'

(Right) Highly successful businessman and new (polo) kid on the block, patron Marek Dochnal, got a good taste of polo when winning the 2004 St. Moritz tournament which is traditionally played in January on the frozen lake. His team consisted of Jack Kidd, Juan Martin Nero and Piki Alberdi. President of the St. Moritz Polo Club, Urs Schwarzenbach, presented the trophy. A delighted Marek expressed his feelings.

'Winning feels great! I love playing polo and we like to win too! I first saw polo a few years ago in Gstaad and told my wife of ten years then that I wanted to play. At first I sponsored a team for the St. Tropez tournament, which the team won. The turning point, however, came when I met Piki Alberdi in September 2003. I told him that I just had to start playing polo! I am very happy because in Piki I have finally found the foundation for my polo operation.'

The FCT team – Jaime Huidobro, Henry Brett, patron Roger Carlsson and Rookie Baillieu – won the 2003 Warwickshire Cup at Cirencester Polo Club beating the Vesteys' Foxcote team.

Jaime really enjoyed playing for FCT. 'Winning one of the high-goal tournaments in England is always a great pleasure, especially when playing with friends.'

Rookie was excited about the win too, particularly as he won it for the second time in succession.

Henry's horses had been late arriving owing to a fire on the road, which Henry found 'quite amusing because this kind of thing always tends to happen to me'.

The Warwickshire Cup is a big one to win, but because it is sandwiched between the Queen's Cup and the Gold Cup, not as many teams enter the tournament as they prefer to save their horses for the Gold Cup.

For patron Roger Carlsson, winning the prestigious Warwickshire Cup was exhilarating.

'It was a lot of fun. The Warwickshire Cup is a good competition with good competitors. Getting into the final already felt good but winning it topped that feeling! We had won the Prince of Wales trophy the year

before in 2002, and so to win another tournament the following season was fabulous. The team worked very well. Jaime took a tumble during the match and I was just very happy that he didn't get injured. I love playing polo. I get fresh air, exercise, excitement and a huge shot of adrenalin from playing!'

Roger and his FCT team didn't play the 2004 season because he was changing yards and didn't get organized in time for the English high-goal season. However, the Swedish patron is planning to be back on the scene, playing for the Queen's Cup and Gold Cup from the 2005 season.

The HB team comprising brothers Ludovic and Sébastien Pailloncy, who took it in turns to play, Mark Tomlinson, Dario Musso and Ernesto Trotz, fought off Royal Barrière in the 2004 Deauville Gold Cup final.

Veteran Ernesto has been playing in Deauville for a long time.

'I have a great relationship with Deauville. I first came here more than twenty years ago and have won the Gold Cup seven times. Winning this time meant a lot because the Pailloncy family are extremely nice! Mr. and Mrs. Pailloncy finance their two sons. The boys are so polite and a joy to be around. I don't only play for the team; I help, train and advise the boys and try to convey my experience to them. For this reason I derived a lot of pleasure from this win! We left it up to the brothers to decide on who was going to play in the final and in the end Sébastian played, which was great because Ludovic had done really well in a couple of tough matches along the way. So winning was really a team effort.'

Mark Tomlinson had played and won in Deauville in 2002 as well as 2003.

'In 2003 I felt that I probably played the best polo of my life. I was in a zone finding it easy to score goals!'

In November 2003 Urs and Francesca Schwarzenbach hosted the tenth Garangula polo tournament on their farm, Garangula, in NSW, Australia. The home team of Urs and Guy Schwarzenbach and New Zealand cousins Simon Keyte and John Paul Clarkin, beat James Packer's Ellerston team.

'The reason I put on this polo tournament is basically for all the people who work there and keep the facilities up to scratch all year round. I enjoy it a lot. We have the best fields in the world, after Ellerston, which makes playing at Garangula a real joy! I have a bit of a bad conscience winning at home because others might think it's a fix!'

JP Clarkin remembers the final as a tough match.

'I think we played well as a team that day. Guy played well and everyone pulled together. In fact, we had not lost a match throughout the tournament. Yet, once you are in the final it can be anyone's game and, luckily, that day it was ours! Winning with "Mr. S." is special. We were all chuffed! It was also the first time Simon and I had played together in Australia.'

Simon Keyte loved the fact that he won the tournament with 'Mister and Master Schwarzenbach'.

'Urs is an exceptional boss. He has a standing joke, which is: whenever he sees me he asks me how old I was when I started to work for him. When I tell him, he then replies "And I still can't get rid of you!" The word that would describe Urs best is "generous" but I am not the only one to have the utmost respect for him. You just have to ask the people who work for him, whether it be his estate managers or polo managers, they all have the hugest respect for him and his wife.'

Patron Guido Boehi's team, Tradition, won the 2004 Sotogrande Gold Cup with players Lolo Castagonola, Alejandro Muzzio and Ignacio Domecq, when playing Michael Redding's Scapa team.

Unusually for southern Spain in August, the final had to be played in moderate to thick fog! Marcos Di Paola, playmaker for Scapa, has been competing in the Gold Cup for four years but says that he had never seen weather like it in Sotogrande before.

'The conditions were bad for both teams so we cannot use it as an excuse for losing. Tradition played well but I think that the match should have been stopped because nobody could see the ball and the third man couldn't make a decision as he couldn't see the play. Tradition *did* play well and I would have loved to have won, especially as this had been the first time I reached the final here.'

Lolo Castagnola on the other hand had won the Gold Cup before. He agrees that it was almost impossible to play but what is important to him is that his team won!

Playing at four, team-mate Ignacio Domecq was very happy too. 'To be playing polo at that level at my age and to win is almost like a miracle!' Ignacio has been in the Gold Cup final fourteen times. Does winning his sixth title in 2004 mean that the scales are perhaps gradually going to balance out?

(Above) Georgie Seddon-Brown presenting the 2004 Warwickshire Cup trophy to Urs Schwarzenbach

(Right) After having won the Warwickshire Cup in 1988, 1991, 1994 and 1997, Urs Schwarzenbach and his Black Bears won it again in 2004. Brothers Javier and Eduardo Novillo-Astrada and Sebastian Dawnay made up the team. For Urs, polo is just like any other day away from work.

'One day I ski, one day I do the Cresta Run and the next I play polo. I don't feel anything special or anything different from when I do the Cresta Run, it is just something to do on a given day. I am not particularly ambitious but that's a bit like saying that I am not superstitious, yet if I see a black cat I would still turn around. Of course I play to win!'

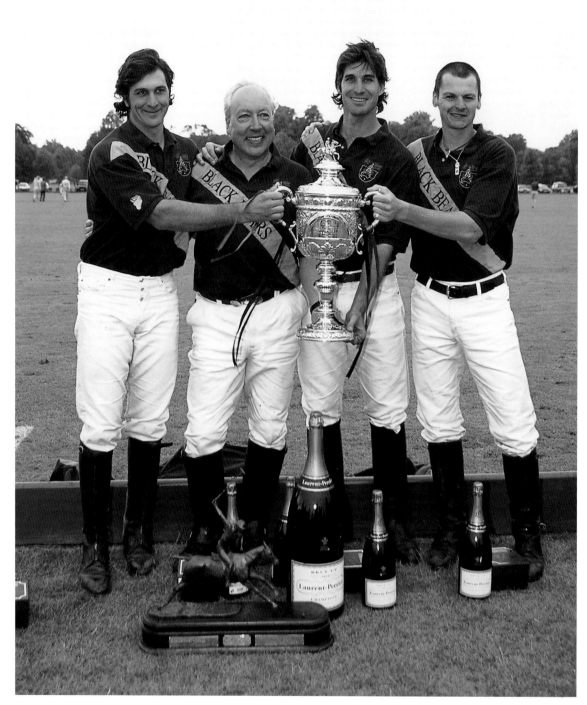

(Above and above right) Ellerston White won the eighteen-goal tournament in Ellerston, Australia. Patron James Packer did not play because of an injury sustained in the previous tournament. Matias MacDonough, John Williams, Andrew Blake Thomas and Gonzalito Pieres beat Wastecorp in the final.

Young English player Andrew Blake Thomas's dream to put on an Ellerston White shirt come true when he was given the chance by Kerry Packer to play the last three matches.

'Winning with the Ellerston White team was by far my greatest and most enjoyable achievement so far. All the horses I played there were Ellerston horses and they were out of this world; they are so well trained and the best horses I have ever ridden.'

Gonzalito Pieres received the trophy for Best Player of the match.

'Receiving the trophy for Best Player is always an honour! I was invited to play for Ellerston because my father had been playing for Kerry Packer for well over ten years. They have a really good relationship and it is thanks to their ongoing friendship that I am lucky enough to be continuing the relationship. Now that my father no longer plays I am keeping up the tradition of playing for Ellerston in Australia and in Argentina.'

Glen Holden, president of the International Polo Federation, is having the time of his life sandwiched between the four ladies polo teams who competed at the 2003 European Championships held in Dallas Burston. England beat Holland in the final. Ireland and Switzerland also competed.

The executive director of the Polo Museum and Hall of Fame, George J. Du Pont (above), stands amongst some of the historical trophies kept at the museum in Lake Worth, Florida.

'At the museum we spend each day preserving yesterday for tomorrow. Getting the trophies back into condition, polishing them and getting the plates on them. However, it's all about the tournament itself and the final!'

A proud moment for John Goodman (right), patron of the 2004 US Open winning team, Isla Carroll. Up on the podium celebrating the win are team-mates Memo Gracida, Pancho Bensadon and Sugar Erskine, and a bunch of children!

The Tedworth team – Edward Nicholson, Sean Wilson-Smith, Bobby Dundas and Edward Magor – won the Gannon section of the 2003 National Pony Club Championship. This championship is traditionally held at Cowdray Park Polo Club.

The Gannon section is the most senior part of the Pony Club Championship. Players have to be under twenty-one on January 1st. It is the only section that gets played over four chukkas and is the closest thing to adult polo. Six teams entered for the final and played for the Daily Telegraph Trophy. Tedworth, a two-goal team, beat Hursley, a one-goal team. The final score was 8–7½.

The Los Locos team of Satnam Dhillon, Mark Tomlinson, Will Lucas and Claire Tomlinson won the 2003 Challenge Cup final, beating the Vampire Bats.

For Claire: 'Playing with Will, Satnam and Mark was a lot of fun. I just love playing with people who can play proper polo. I don't like playing with people who lose their cool! The fascinating thing about polo is that there are so many skills involved: the horsemanship encompasses schooling the horse, getting it right for the actual game, plus the breeding side; and then there is the ball skill and the team play; I absolutely love team sports.'

(Right) Alfio Marchini and his team Loro Piana-Terranova won the subsidiary final for the Sotogrande Gold Cup. Their match against home team Santa Maria-Graffham was played in foggy conditions before the actual final of the Gold Cup which was played when the fog was even thicker. Owing to the delays, both prize-giving ceremonies were held quite late. Nonetheless, Alfio and his son Alessandro saw the funny side of having to wait until the end of the day before being handed this rather lovely trophy.

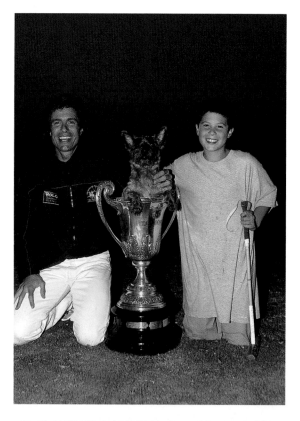

(Above) Black Bears patron, Urs Schwarzenbach, and Hubert Perrodo, patron of Labegorce, with their respective trophies. Hubert won the 2004 Queen's Cup and Urs the subsidiary of the Queen's Cup.

'Ideally polo should be played amongst friends. During the late 1980s and early nineties there was a good camaraderie between teams. We would even spend time together outside polo but this almost disappeared from the mid-nineties onwards. I don't really know why; perhaps because polo has become more competitive. Hubert and I are good friends and I am just as happy when he wins as when I win, even if he is playing against me.'

(Left) England qualified for the 2004 World Championships by winning the 2003 European league held in Dallas Burston. Captain Antony Fanshawe played with Tom Morley, James Beim and George Merrick.

England met Italy in the final. James puts their win down to having followed coach Claire Tomlinson's advice.

'Claire did really well for us. She gave us a great game plan, which we stuck to and it worked!'

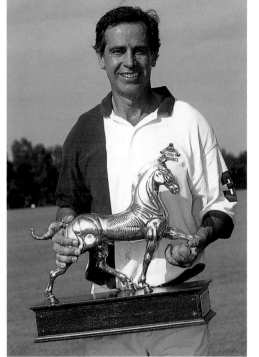

Keeping it in the family! Weston Gracida (far right), son of Mexican Reubens Gracida, who is Carlos's and Memo's cousin, received the trophy for best young, up-and-coming polo player during the 2004 Florida season. He will no doubt one day also have his name engraved on some of the major polo trophies.

Carlos Gracida (right) was beginning to think that winning the Queen's Cup would elude him for ever when Labegorce lost the 2003 final by the narrowest margins to Dubai. Carlos's disappointment was too great to have been consoled by receiving the trophy for Best Player of the match.

'In my entire career I think I have probably lost two or three matches through the fault of the umpires, and this final was one of them. It was such a massive disappointment I can't even describe it. At the end of the game a huge foul was committed just in front of the goal. I was very upset, particularly because it happened in the finals of the Queen's Cup and I couldn't believe that there was yet another thing that would prevent me from winning this title! Had we lost owing to my mistake or the mistake of one of my team-mates, it would not have mattered as much, but I was actually happy with the way I played. When you play against Adolfo, who is the best player in the world, and you get the Best Player award, it's nice, sure, no doubt about it, but I would have preferred to win the title.'

Fortunately, Carlos only had to wait twelve months before he finally was able to lift the Queen's Cup!

Patrick Guerrand-Hermès, president of the Chantilly Polo Club, who hosted the 2004 World Championships. A keen player in his day, Patrick shows just as much enthusiasm and love for the game now as he ever has.

After a ten-year gap, Black Bears managed to win the Veuve Cliquot Gold Cup for the second time. Patron Urs Schwarzenbach remembers one or two things that helped along the way.

'The 2002 win was very special because we were actually not meant to have reached the final. During our quarter-final match against FCT we were three goals down in the sixth chukka with two and a half minutes to go. We were very lucky to score a goal and then to avoid a goal from FCT. Next, we got awarded a penalty that we converted and then we scored another goal to equalize. This took us into overtime and we scored in the first minute! Winning that match was sheer luck, especially as it was a low-scoring match. We had only managed to score four goals in five and a half chukkas, and then to score three goals in the last two minutes of the sixth to take us into overtime was quite something! Well, understandably, FCT was not very happy. Tommy Llorente's wife came up and said that we had had all the luck in the Gold Cup and that from now on we really had to start playing polo! And that is exactly what we did. We beat Dubai in the semi-final and then beat Emerging in the final!

'We scored the winning goal in the last ten seconds, but it was slightly different because we had actually been leading by one or two goals all the way and somehow the two-goal lead slipped away in the last chukka. Yet, I somehow never felt that we would lose. Of course we could have, which only dawned on me after the match. We did dominate the game however.

'We felt especially good after having beaten Dubai in the semi-final because one always has this idea about Cambiaso being able to do everything and anything, which he can't because he is only human after all!'

The Cowdray Park winners of the 2003 Jack Gannon Cup, a subsidiary of the Veuve Cliquot Gold Cup. Team members José Donoso, Lila Pearson, Gabriel Donoso and Mauricio Devrient-Kidd are all smiles!

To be playing for Cowdray Park and being in a team with his brother José and friends Lila and Mauricio was 'very meaningful' for Gabriel.

(Left) Italian Patron Stefano Marsaglia started playing high-goal polo in 2002. His 2004 season turned into 'a dream come true'. In June, Azzurra reached the final of the Queen's Cup but lost, by only a narrow margin, to Labegorce. In July they beat Dubai impressively, 17–9 , in a match in which Stefano and his team members – Marcos Heguy, Juan Martin Nero and Alejandro 'Negro' Novilla-Astrada – all played outstanding polo! Juan Martin, who had already gone up by a handicap after the Queen's Cup final, was put up by a further goal after their win. He is now playing off handicap nine in England. Alejandro was put up to six and Marcos, already a ten-goal player, was truly on fire and was most certainly playing above his handicap too.

As for Stefano, well, he scored, and he admitted after the match, 'I get quite excited when I score because it doesn't happen very often!'

Juan Martin remembers that when he was asked to play for Azzurra he dreamed of winning the Gold Cup.

'So when it actually happened I could hardly believe it! Having gone up to nine, however, has almost put an end to my playing in England as it is going to be really difficult to find a team. I am happy in one way but quite frankly I don't regard myself as a nine-goal player. If I think of a nine-goal player I look at Gonzalito Pieres and the Novillo-Astradas, and I don't consider myself being in their league.'

(Right) The very young Hildon Sport team – the Tomlinson brothers, Luke and Mark, JP Clarkin and Nina Vestey – delighted many by winning the 2003 Veuve Cliquot Gold Cup.

The four players started to believe it was possible to win when they reached the final by beating the favourite, Dubai, in the semi-final.

JP Clarkin has these memories of the game.

'We had been talking about putting a team together for the 2003 season the winter before. To have really done it with three good friends was fantastic! The friendship helped us to get through the inevitable ups and down we encountered during the season, particularly after our performance during the Queen's Cup. No one could have possibly picked us to win the Gold Cup, but luckily Claire Tomlinson and Milo Fernandez-Araujo coached us from the quarter-finals onwards and it just all came together. We certainly believed that if we played well enough we could do it and, fortunately, with the bit of luck one also needs along the way, we did do it. It was a great feeling; one that no one can ever take away from us. For me, to win the Gold Cup when having the first crack at it was quite surreal, especially knowing that people have tried for years and never got close!'

Nina remembers having been 'amazingly nervous'.

'We had already beaten Labegorce 16–15 in a league match to get into the quarter-finals. Playing them again in the final suddenly made the possibility of beating them again and winning the Gold Cup seem real. One of my horses felt rather tired and it became quite nerve-wracking. However, we went into the match with a huge amount of determination and were very focused. Having Claire, Milo and Tim Keyte there made a huge difference.'

Renato Diniz-Junqueira, is the younger of two brothers who played for Brazil during the 2004 World Championships. He rode the pony that was awarded Best Pony of the match in the semi-final against the home nation, France.

Chile finished in third place at the 2004 World Championships held at the beginning of September in Chantilly. Playmaker for the Chilean team was Alejandro Vial who was also a member of the victorious Chilean team that beat England in the Coronation Cup in July of the same year.

(Left) England players Andrew Blake Thomas, Matt Lodder, captain Tom Morley and James Harper, fought a good match against Chile at the 2004 World Championships, which helped them clinch a deserved victory. Coach Claire Tomlinson had to suffer a few hairy moments towards the end of the match when Chile looked like closing in.

'Our boys played a really disciplined game and kept cool heads. A bit of inexperience let them down occasionally but all in all they followed instructions. They were not as relaxed hitting the ball as they could have been.'

(Right) Urs Schwarzenbach's Black Bears started their 2004 English season in style with a win in the Indian Empire Challenge Shield, an eighteen-goal tournament they used as a warm-up for the high goal that was still to come. On the team were Sebastian Dawnay, Nicolas Antinori. Brothers Javier (pictured) and Eduardo Novillo-Astrada played in alternate matches.

Nicolas, younger brother of Vieri Antinori, was asked by Javier at the end of the 2003 season whether he wanted to play with Black Bears.

'I have always wanted to play for one of the big teams and so to have been asked to play for Black Bears was a big honour! To win in the first tournament I played with them was amazing! We had a very good team and the organization at Black Bears is simply great!

'I only entered the tournament because I wanted a replica of this incredible trophy! We used the tournament primarily as a warm-up for the two number four players, Sebastian and Nicolas. It is more fun to have something to play for instead of only playing practice chukkas!'

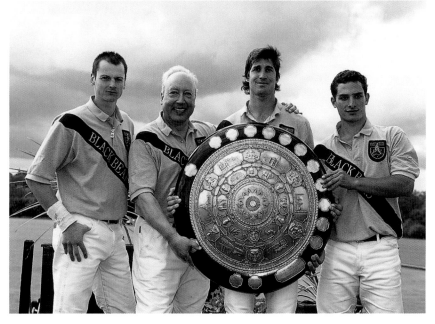

Tom Morley, Dallas
Burston 2003.

LASTING
IMPRESSIONS

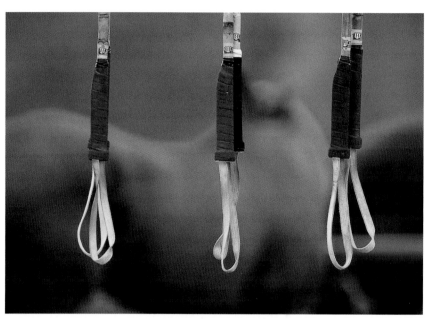

(Clockwise from above)

Cartier International, 2003.

Deauville 2003.

US Open 2004.

(Clockwise from right)

Guards 2003.

Cowdray 2003

Guards 2003.

Guards 2004.

(Above) England 2003.

(Above left) Cowdray 2003.

(Top) Guards 2004.

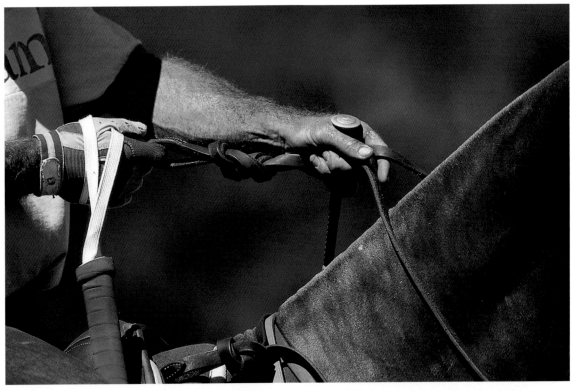

(Clockwise from above)

St. Moritz 2004.

Ellerston 2004.

Guards 2004.

A wheelbarrow-load of tack,
Shiplake 2004.

(Far left) Passing a cup of *mate* back to its owner, Matias MacDonough, Cowdray 2004.

(Left) Jaime Le Hardy, Ellerston 2004.

(Below) Guards 2003.

Ellerston 2004.

Cowdray 2003.

(Above) Deauville 2003,
Benedicte Pailloncy,
patron of HB polo team

Ellerston 2004.

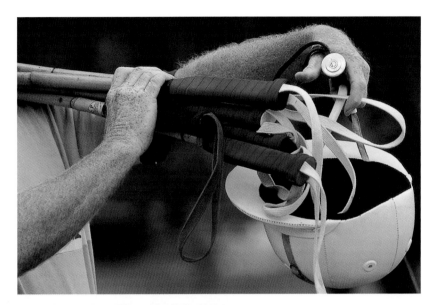

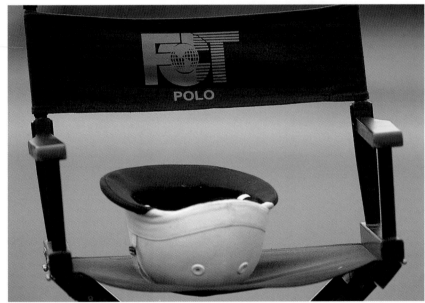

(Above) Cirencester 2003.

(Top) Ellerston 2004.

(Right) Memo Gracida, US Open 2004.

(Above) Ham Polo Club 2004.

(Top) James Harper, Cirencester 2003.

(Left) Pite Merlos, US Open 2004.

(Right) Roger Carlsson,
Cirencester 2003.

(Far right) FCT pony,
Cirencester 2003.

(Below) JP Clarkin,
Guards 2003.

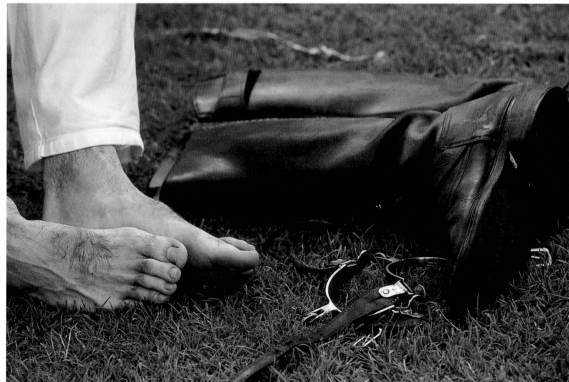

(Above) Talandracas mascot, Deauville 2003.

(Top left) Oakland Park pony line, Cowdray 2003.

(Top right) Deauville 2003.

(Left) Bautista Heguy stretching, Guards 2004.

Glen Gilmore, Ellerston 2004.

(Right) Urs Schwarzenbach, patron of Black Bears before the Veuve Cliquot Gold Cup final 2002; Black Bears beat Emerging.

(Far right) Pepe Heguy's final preparation before the Queen's Cup final 2003.

(Left) Guillermo Terrera changing ponies in mid-chukka, Queen's Cup 2003.

(Above) John Paul Clarkin, Garangula 2003.

(Right) HRH Prince Harry
and Mark Tomlinson happy
to have won the 2003
Golden Jubilee Cup.

(Below right) Gerardo 'Toto'
Collardin being comforted
by his wife after losing the
quarter-finals of the Gold
Cup 2003.

(Below) Pancho Bensadon
getting congratulated after
winning the US Open 2004.

Marcos Heguy and Andrea
Vianini discussing matters
after a league match of the
2004 Veuve Cliquot Gold Cup.

Javier Novillo-Astrada skilfully
catching his patron's horse;
they had parted company!

INDEX

LUKE TOMLINSON

PABLO SPINACCI

JACK 'ROOKIE' BAILLIEU

NACHO GONZALEZ

CARINA VESTEY

NICHOLAS ANTINORI

LUDOVIC CRESSANT

SANTIAGO CHAVANNE

JAIME HUIDOBRO

IGNACIO NOVILLO ASTRADA

FERNANDO REYNOT

JAVIER NOVILLO ASTRADA

GLEN A. GILMORE

PABLO MACDONOUGH

SANTIAGO V. GAZTAMBIDE

ADOLFO CAMBIASO

EDOUARD CARMIGNAC

PAUL M. WITHERS

DAVID 'PELON' STIRLING

GILLIAN JOHNSTON

TARIQ ALBWARDY

ANDREW C. HINE

URS E. SCHWARZENBACH

FRANCISCO 'PANCHO'
BENSADON

S.S. DHILLON

TIM KEYTE

TOMAS FERNANDEZ LLORENTE

ERNESTO TROTZ

HERNAN AGOTE

IGNACIO TILLOUS

ROBERT THAME

EMMA TOMLINSON